A
DIVINE
REVELATION
OF
HEAVEN

A
DIVINE
REVELATION
OF
HEAVEN

MARY K. BAXTER
WITH DR. T. L. LOWERY

Whitaker House

A DIVINE REVELATION OF HEAVEN

Mary K. Baxter with Dr. T. L. Lowery
Lowery Ministries International
P. O. Box 54095
Washington, D.C. 20032

ISBN: 0-88368-524-8
Printed in the United States of America
Copyright © 1998 by Lowery Ministries International

Whitaker House
30 Hunt Valley Circle
New Kensington, PA 15068

Library of Congress Cataloging-in-Publication Data

Baxter, Mary K.
    A divine revelation of heaven / Mary K. Baxter, with T. L. Lowery.
        p.   cm.
    ISBN 0-88368-524-8 (trade paper : alk. paper)
    1. Heaven—Christianity. 2. Private revelations. 3. Visions.
4. Baxter, Mary K.   I. Lowery, T. L. (Thomas Lanier), 1929–
II. Title.
BT848.B34   1998
236'.24—dc21   98-24168

1 2 3 4 5 6 7 8 9 10 11 12 / 07 06 05 04 03 02 01 00 99 98

To give praise, honor,
and glory to God,
this book is dedicated to

The Father,

The Son,

and

The Holy Spirit.

Contents

Foreword

The inspired writings of Mary Kathryn Baxter are divinely anointed by God, and they have blessed hundreds of thousands of people. I believe it is of utmost importance to widely disseminate the message that God has given to her. She shares these experiences in hundreds of churches each year, and she has now put them down in book form.

Her previous book, *A Divine Revelation of Hell,* has been especially used of God to deliver the eternal message of salvation to the lost. It has been widely received with enthusiasm by people all over the world, having been printed in many different countries and in many different languages. Well over half a million copies have been sold to date. I believe this book, *A Divine*

Revelation of Heaven, will be received in an even greater way.

As Mary Kathryn Baxter's pastor for several years, I know her personally, and I fully endorse her ministry. God has placed His approval on her work by anointing her ministry and by giving this message such a wide acceptance.

This book is the result of many prayers, tears, and hard work. I pray that its wide distribution will be the cause of many souls coming to know the Lord and making preparations to spend eternity in heaven!

—*T. L. Lowery, Ph.D.*

Introduction

This book is an account of a number of true experiences I have had with God. It is not the work of an overactive imagination or the pipe dream of someone who hopes for something better than this life has to offer.

Heaven is a reality, and the experiences I describe in this book are told just as they happened to me. I did not see everything there is to see in heaven—it will take eternity to do that. I do not relate everything I saw in heaven; even Paul did not do that. (See 2 Corinthians 12:1–4.) But I am relating all that God has told me to share.

I want to give special honor and thanks to my pastor, the Reverend Dr. T. L. Lowery, and to his beautiful wife, Mildred, for their support, encouragement, and valuable contributions in this endeavor. I also would like to express my sincere gratitude for the staff of the National Church of God and for the Reverend Marcus V. Hand for his editorial guidance on this book. Additionally, I gratefully recognize and credit all those at Whitaker House in New Kensington, Pennsylvania, who have been instrumental in so many ways in making both *A Divine Revelation of Heaven* and *A Divine Revelation of Hell* available to the reading public.

I am grateful to God who has called me to share this message. I thank you who have strengthened and encouraged me in my God-called ministry. God bless you all!

—*Mary K. Baxter*

TO KATHRYN FROM JESUS

For this purpose you were born,
to write and tell
what I have shown and told you,
for these things are faithful and true.
Your call is to let the world know
that there is a heaven,
that there is a hell,
and that I, Jesus, was sent by the Father
to save them from torment
and to prepare them a place in heaven.

One

Inside the Gates

God, in His infinite mercy and grace, permitted me to go to that beautiful place called heaven. The logistics of my trip to His home and back to earth are unclear to me, but I cannot be mistaken about the reality of it.

How were the incomparable wonders of heaven revealed to a mere mortal like me? Let me start at the beginning.

One night the Lord appeared to me and told me I was chosen for a special assignment.

He said, "My child, I will manifest Myself to you to bring people out of darkness into light. I have chosen you for a purpose: you are to write and make a record of the things that I will show and tell you."

I submitted myself to God completely, and astounding things began to happen. I was taken from where I was at the time and transported into hell itself. I was aware of all five of my senses: I could see, feel, hear, smell, and taste. Yet, this was a supernatural happening. I realized that the impact it made on me was for a purpose.

For days after I was taken by the Lord into hell, I was very grieved in my heart. My heart was sad and burdened because of the horrors I saw. I had viewed the judgment of God on sin and on the people who had gone to hell. I prayed earnestly to God and sought His comfort.

On the thirty-first night after these events began, the power of Almighty God fell on me again. At two o'clock in the morning, a mighty angel stood beside my bed. Jesus Christ was standing behind the angel. As I looked on the face of the Lord standing there, He smiled at me, but He did not say anything.

The mighty messenger of God said, "God has given me a special mission. I am sent here to take you to heaven and to show you parts of it."

After a moment, he spoke again, "Come and see the glory of God!"

At once, I was supernaturally transported from my home and found myself standing outside one of the gates of heaven with the heavenly angel.

The overwhelming beauty of what I saw around me was breathtaking! The clothing the heavenly being wore looked like a brilliant garment of light. The angel had triangular-shaped wings that glistened with the colors of the rainbow. Although I wasn't surprised, I was amazed at the indescribable beauty of God that was evident all around.

The next thing I knew, the angel repeated an exclamation that I would hear many times: "Behold, the glory of God!"

The magnificent gate that stood before me in splendor was made of a solid pearl. In awe I took in everything I could of this most beautiful sight. At this point, I could not see the Lord anywhere, but I was totally enraptured by the glory of heaven.

ENTERING HEAVEN

When we arrived there, two very tall angels were standing outside the gate. Both of them wore glistening robes and had swords in their hands. Their hair was like spun gold, and their faces gleamed with light.

The angel accompanying me moved over to speak to the two angels guarding the gate, and I was left standing alone. In amazement, I thought, "Oh, how glorious are the gates of heaven! How wonderful it is to see this one for myself!" Suddenly, I realized that I was actually going to enter into heaven.

As I watched the angels of the Lord, I could hear some of the conversation they were having. One of them went inside the gate and returned almost immediately with a small volume. The book had a gold cover, and the printing inside was also in gold. It seemed to be a book about my life's history. My name was stamped on the cover:

Mary Kathryn Baxter

A smile of approval came over the angels' faces. They opened the book. They looked at each other, then said in a voice I could hear, "She may come inside the gate."

My guiding angel escorted me through the magnificent gate and into heaven.

Suddenly, music filled the whole atmosphere. It was all around me. It was above me. It seemed to penetrate my very being. Wave after powerful wave of beautiful music and singing surged across the landscape and seemed to envelop everything and everyone.

When I stepped inside the city, amazement again took my breath. The landscape of that incomparable city was beyond description. Surrounding me were the most beautiful, colorful flowers I had ever seen. There was unbelievable greenery and vegetation everywhere. Even the blooms of the flowers seemed to be alive to the music and the singing.

Music continued to swirl about me. I seemed to be a part of it.

It is one thing to try to describe the wonders of this city; it is quite another to know that you will share the joy of it.

I saw some of the exuberant citizens of heaven, and they were all dressed in robes. This Scripture came to me:

> 10 *I will greatly rejoice in the LORD; my soul shall be joyful in my God; for He has clothed me with the garments of salvation, He has covered me with the robe of righteousness, as a bridegroom decks himself with ornaments, and as a bride adorns herself with her jewels.*
>
> (Isaiah 61:10)

The happiness and joy that beamed from their faces was beyond compare.

Heaven is a real place. It is not a figment of someone's imagination. In the Bible it is recorded that Jesus said,

> 1 *Let not your heart be troubled; you believe in God, believe also in Me.*
> 2 *In My Father's house are many mansions; if it were not so, I would have*

told you. I go to prepare a place for you.
(John 14:1–2)

Heaven is a prepared place for a prepared people. Since we as children of God have been transformed and made new by the miracle of regeneration, and since we are now new creations in Christ, it is a joy to know that the place where we will spend eternity is prepared by the Savior who saved us.

Heaven is a perfect place. Since our Savior is perfect, omnipotent, and eternal, heaven has to be a perfect place. Because He is preparing us a place there to live with Him for all eternity, our eternal home will be perfect, too. Nothing will ever mar any part of that heavenly abode. There will never be anything allowed to enter heaven to defile it or spoil it.

> [27] *But there shall by no means enter it anything that defiles, or causes an abomination or a lie, but only those who are written in the Lamb's Book of Life.*
> (Revelation 21:27)

Heaven is beyond the reach of sin and sinners of every kind and description. Satan will be forever barred from that heavenly place:

> [3] *And another sign appeared in heaven: behold, a great, fiery red dragon having seven heads and ten horns, and seven diadems on his heads.*
> [4] *His tail drew a third of the stars [angelic hosts] of heaven and threw them to the earth. And the dragon stood before the woman who was ready to give birth, to devour her Child as soon as it was born.*
> [7] *And war broke out in heaven: Michael and his angels fought with the dragon; and the dragon and his angels fought,*
> [8] *but they did not prevail, nor was a place found for them in heaven any longer.*
> [9] *So the great dragon was cast out, that serpent of old, called the Devil and Satan, who deceives the whole world; he was cast to the earth, and his angels were cast out with him.*
> [10] *Then I heard a loud voice saying in heaven, "Now salvation, and strength, and the kingdom of our God, and the power of His Christ have come, for the accuser of our brethren, who accused them before our God day and night, has been cast down.*

^{12} *"Therefore rejoice, O heavens, and you who dwell in them! Woe to the inhabitants of the earth and the sea! For the devil has come down to you, having great wrath, because he knows that he has a short time."*
^{13} *Now when the dragon saw that he had been cast to the earth, he persecuted the woman who gave birth to the male Child.*
(Revelation 12:3–4, 7–10, 12–13)

That serpent, Satan, and his unholy cohorts will never again rear their ugly heads in the pure and holy climate of heaven!

The demons cannot enter heaven. The fallen angels who rebelled against God and *"who did not keep their proper domain, but left their own abode"* (Jude 1:6) cannot return to heaven.

Nothing will be lacking in heaven. No detail will be left out to keep its environment from being perfect.

No matter where we go on earth, no matter where we live or how expensive our homes may be, there are obvious faults and flaws to keep them from being perfect. In contrast, God has made no mistakes in constructing the place called heaven. Its glories, its beauties, its wonders are beyond human powers of description. The indescribable splendor of that beautiful place is wondrous to behold.

The combined brilliance of the light of the Son of God reflecting on walls of jasper, gates of pearl, mansions unnumbered, and the beautiful River of Life creates a scene no artist could ever adequately depict.

HOME OF REDEEMED SOULS

Heaven is a permanent place. No enemy will ever conquer the paradise of God. There will be no crumbling of its buildings, no decay of its materials, and no withering or dying of its vegetation. No smog or radiation will ever pollute its holy atmosphere.

This permanent, abiding place is an eternal, continuing city. We sing this song, written by Hattie Buell:

A tent or a cottage, why should I care?
    They're building a palace for me over there;
Tho' exiled from Him, yet still I may sing;
    All glory to God, I'm a child of the King.

In that incomparable place, saints will find sweet deliverance from all disappointments, heartaches, tragedies, and disasters. There will be no more sorrow or woe. There will be no more pain. There will be no more crying:

> ⁴ *And God will wipe away every tear from their eyes; there shall be no more death, nor sorrow, nor crying. There shall be no more pain, for the former things have passed away.*   (Revelation 21:4)

The joyful citizens I saw in heaven seemed to have come from many different ages and countries. Various nationalities seemed obvious to me. Then I remembered another Scripture I had read:

> ⁹ *And they sang a new song, saying: "You are worthy to take the scroll, and to open its seals; for You were slain, and have redeemed us to God by Your blood out of every tribe and tongue and people and nation."*   (Revelation 5:9)

EMPLOYED IN PRAISING GOD

Excitedly, my soul praised the majesty of God! The sorrows I experienced and the grief I suffered when I saw a revelation of hell now seemed so far away. This was a revelation of heaven.

I saw entire families together. Everybody was happy, going somewhere, doing something, smiling. A glow graced every face I saw.

All the saints in heaven seemed to be occupied. They were constantly busy. They spent their time praising and magnifying God. Songs were on everyone's lips. The atmosphere of music was the dominant mood.

Eternity will not be spent in leisure and laziness, as some have mistakenly pictured our final destination. We will do more than float on a cloud, strum a harp, or wiggle our toes in the River of Life. Our time will be occupied in service to God. Just what the nature of this service will be, we cannot say, but there can be no doubt that His people will serve Him.

DIAMONDS FOR SOULWINNERS

I could see diamonds—glittering, glistening, exquisite diamonds—diamonds everywhere! Some were are as large as blocks of concrete.

Some of these diamonds seemed to be for the mansions of those who were soulwinners on earth. It seemed that every time someone led a soul to Christ, heaven provided a diamond for that faithful Christian. The Bible says,

> [30] *The fruit of the righteous is a tree of life, and he who wins souls is wise.*
>
> (Proverbs 11:30)

> [3] *Those who are wise shall shine like the brightness of the firmament, and those who turn many to righteousness like the stars forever and ever.*
>
> (Daniel 12:3)

As I stood drinking in the splendor and grandeur of that glorious place, I saw an immense, beautiful angel coming down a path. In his hands he held a scroll, which had gold edging on it.

The angel laid the scroll on a pedestal table, which was made of a silvery material unlike anything I had ever seen before. The oblong table literally glistened with light.

The scroll had a name written on it. One of the saints picked it up and began to read it.

"Jesus is the Master Builder," a saint in heaven told me. "He determines who deserves the diamonds and where they go. This scroll I hold is a report from earth of a person who has led someone to Jesus, who fed the poor, who clothed the naked—who did great things for God."

31 *When the Son of Man comes in His glory, and all the holy angels with Him, then He will sit on the throne of His glory.*

32 *All the nations will be gathered before Him, and He will separate them one from another, as a shepherd divides his sheep from the goats.*

33 *And He will set the sheep on His right hand, but the goats on the left.*

34 *Then the King will say to those on His right hand, "Come, you blessed of My Father, inherit the kingdom prepared for you from the foundation of the world:*

35 *"for I was hungry and you gave Me food; I was thirsty and you gave Me drink; I was a stranger and you took Me in;*

36 *"I was naked and you clothed Me; I was sick and you visited Me; I was in*

prison and you came to Me."
37 Then the righteous will answer Him,
saying, "Lord, when did we see You
hungry and feed You, or thirsty and
give You drink?
38 "When did we see You a stranger and
take You in, or naked and clothe You?
39 "Or when did we see You sick, or in
prison, and come to You?"
40 And the King will answer and say to
them, "Assuredly, I say to you, inas-
much as you did it to one of the least of
these My brethren, you did it to Me."
41 Then He will also say to those on the
left hand, "Depart from Me, you cursed,
into the everlasting fire prepared for the
devil and his angels.
46 "And these will go away into everlast-
ing punishment, but the righteous into
eternal life."   (Matthew 25:31–41, 46)

ROOM FOR EVERYBODY

The angel repeated the welcome theme to
me: "Come and see the glory of your God."

At the Lord's direction, I am recording this
account of heaven as I saw it. We need to understand that the focus of our hopes and desires
should be to spend all eternity with our Lord.

Heaven is the land of dreams come true!

I'm excited about heaven because after our works and labors on earth are finished, we will leave this earth and go there. God has prepared the city, and Jesus is preparing a place there for those of us who love Him.

PERFECT COMMUNION

Unbroken fellowship between God and man will be completely restored in heaven.

When Adam and Eve were in the Garden of Eden, God paid visits to this earth. After fellowship with Him was broken by sin and disobedience, God continued to show His desire for communion with mankind.

His ultimate expression of love for mankind was the giving of His own Son to die a merciless death on a cruel cross. Through Christ's death and resurrection, fellowship between God and man again became a possibility.

Even now, the circumstances of life can hinder our intimate fellowship with God. But, in heaven there will be no more hindrances. We will know perfect fellowship with the King of

Kings and the Lord of Lords. Fellowship with Him will be complete.

Heaven is the abode of the living God. It is far above the atmospheric heavens and beyond the planets and galaxies. It is the everlasting home of *"The Redeemed of the LORD"* (Isaiah 62:12). It is the eternal destination of all the children of God through faith in Christ.

You do not need to fear being crowded into a tiny cubicle in heaven that has been labeled a "mansion." When the redeemed of the ages are gathered home to glory, there will be sufficient room for all of them to have one of the many mansions, the many dwelling places, which Jesus said He was preparing for us in His Father's house:

> [1] *Let not your heart be troubled; you believe in God, believe also in Me.*
> [2] *In My Father's house are many mansions; if it were not so, I would have told you. I go to prepare a place for you.*
> [3] *And if I go and prepare a place for you, I will come again and receive you to Myself; that where I am, there you may be also.*

*⁴ And where I go you know, and the way
you know.*   (John 14:1–4)

Heaven definitely has room for everyone:

*⁹ After these things I looked, and be-
hold, a great multitude which no one
could number, of all nations, tribes,
peoples, and tongues, standing before
the throne and before the Lamb, clothed
with white robes, with palm branches in
their hands,*
*¹⁰ and crying out with a loud voice, say-
ing, "Salvation belongs to our God who
sits on the throne, and to the Lamb!"*
*¹¹ All the angels stood around the
throne and the elders and the four living
creatures, and fell on their faces before
the throne and worshiped God.*
                    (Revelation 7:9–11)

TEARS IN HEAVEN

At one point I was taken to a particular
place where the angel stopped and said to me,
"God wants me to show you the room of tears."

Many times you may have read in several
passages in the Psalms about our tears and
about how God cares for us. The angels catch

our tears and put them in bottles (Psalm 56:8). Many times I had wondered about what this meant.

I know that many of you reading these words have cried many tears for your loved ones, your children, your mate, or your family. Especially if you've gone through a separation or a divorce, you have felt like all hope was gone. You have grieved over your lost loved ones.

I want to tell you that God showed me a room of tears. It was so beautiful. The angel took me to a grand entranceway that had no door.

Looking inside, I could see that the room itself wasn't large, but the holiness and power radiating from it amazed me. Lined with crystal shelves, the inside walls glowed with light.

On the shelves were many bottles, some of which were in clusters of three and looked like clear glass. Under each sparkling cluster of glass-like bottles was a plaque with a name on it. There were many of these bottles in the room.

Then inside the room I saw a man who appeared to have been glorified. His deep purple robe was very beautiful and looked like velvet.

An elegant table, which was made of a rich-looking material and glowed with majestic splendor, was just inside the door. The lavish display I saw astonished me!

Books were lying on the table, and they looked as if they were sewn in the most beautiful silk-like material I have ever seen. Some had diamonds, pearls, and lace on them; others had green and purple stones on them. All of them were intricately made.

I thought to myself, "Oh, God, how beautiful these books are!" I love books. These books especially appealed to me. They were stunning. As I gazed about, I was overcome with wonder.

At this point the man in the room said to me, "Come and see. I want to show you this room, and I want to explain to you about tears. This is only one of many rooms like it. I am in charge of this room."

As he talked, a large angel came through the entranceway. The beauty and majesty of this heavenly being astounded me. I noticed that he wore a white, glistening garment with gold-edged trim that went all the way down the front. He seemed to be about twelve feet tall and had very large wings.

The angel held a small bowl in his hands. The golden bowl was filled (see Revelation 5:8) with a liquid. The man in the room told me, "He has just brought me a bowl of tears from the earth. I want you to see what we do with this."

The angel handed him the bowl, along with a piece of paper. The note held the name of the person whose tears were in the bowl.

The man in the room read the note and then went over to one of the places where the bottles were kept. He read the plaque under the bottle, and I knew it matched the person from earth who was named in the note.

The man picked up the bottle that was nearly full and brought it over to the bowl. He poured the tears from the golden bowl into the bottle.

"I want to show you what we do here," the man said to me. "Tell the people on earth about this." Then he took the bottle over to the table, picked up one of the books, opened it, and said, "Look!"

The pages in the book were completely blank. The keeper of the room said to me, "These are tears from the saints of God on earth as they cry to God. See what happens."

Then the man poured a drop from the bottle, one little teardrop, on the first page of the book. When he did, words began to appear immediately. Beautiful words, elegantly handwritten, started appearing on the page. Each time a tear fell on a page, a whole page of writing appeared. He continued doing this page after page, time and time again.

As he closed the book and spoke, he seemed to be saying to all humanity as well as to me, "The most perfect prayers are those that are bathed in tears that come from the hearts and souls of men and women on earth."

Then the angel with rainbow wings said to me, "Come and see the glory of God."

GOD OPENED THE BOOK

Immediately, we were transported to a huge place with thousands and thousands of people and heavenly beings. Oh, it was beautiful!

In a little while the people seemed to fade away, and an even greater display of God's glory began to appear everywhere. The high praises of God became thunderous.

The angelic messenger took me to the throne of God.

I saw a huge cloud, a mist, and I saw an image of the Being in the cloud. I could not see God's face, but I saw the glory of God and a rainbow over the throne. I heard the voice of God, and it sounded to me just as John described it: *"I heard a voice from heaven, like the voice of many waters, and like the voice of loud thunder"* (Revelation 14:2). In this mighty arena, I saw many horses with riders beside the throne.

Suddenly, I saw a book lying on the huge altar in front of God's throne. I saw angels bowing before Him. Standing in awe, I watched this scene, and I saw what looked like a man's hand come out of the cloud and open up the book.

Somehow I knew it was the hand of God that opened the book.

Amazed, I saw what looked like smoke ascending from the book. Suddenly, the most beautiful perfume I ever smelled filled the whole area where I stood. The angel told me that this book contains the prayers of the saints and that God was sending His angels to earth to answer the prayers from the cries of their hearts. Everybody was praising and magnifying God.

As God opened up the book, pages began to come out of the volume and fly into the hands of the angels on the horses. I could hear His voice, *"like the voice of loud thunder,"* shouting and saying, "Go, answer her prayers! Go, answer his prayers!"

> 8 *You number my wanderings;*
> *Put my tears into Your bottle;*
> *Are they not in Your book?*
> 9 *When I cry out to You,*
> *Then my enemies will turn back;*
> *This I know, because God is for me.*
> 10 *In God (I will praise His word),*
> *In the LORD (I will praise His word),*
> 11 *In God I have put my trust;*
> *I will not be afraid.*
> *What can man do to me?*
> (Psalm 56:8–11)

The living Word of God explains to us what He does with our tears. How beautiful it is to understand the glory and the wonder of our God! How marvelous it is to be recipients of His compassion! He cares even about our tears.

Many Scriptures speak to us about our tears, about our sorrows, and about God's comfort for us. Read these and rejoice:

> [5] *Thus says the LORD, the God of David your father: "I have heard your prayer, I have seen your tears; surely I will heal you."*　　　　　(2 Kings 20:5)

> [6] *I am weary with my groaning; all night I make my bed swim; I drench my couch with my tears.*
> [7] *My eye wastes away because of grief; it grows old because of all my enemies.*
> [8] *Depart from me, all you workers of iniquity; for the LORD has heard the voice of my weeping.*
> [9] *The LORD has heard my supplication; The LORD will receive my prayer.*
> 　　　　　　　　　　　　(Psalm 6:6–9)

> [8] *For You have delivered my soul from death, my eyes from tears, and my feet from falling.*　　　　(Psalm 116:8)

⁵ Those who sow in tears shall reap in joy. ⁶ He who continually goes forth weeping, bearing seed for sowing, shall doubtless come again with rejoicing, bringing his sheaves with him.

(Psalm 126:5–6)

⁸ He will swallow up death forever, and the Lord GOD will wipe away tears from all faces. (Isaiah 25:8)

¹⁶ Refrain your voice from weeping, and your eyes from tears; for your work shall be rewarded, says the LORD, and they shall come back from the land of the enemy. (Jeremiah 31:16)

¹⁷ The Lamb who is in the midst of the throne will shepherd them and lead them to living fountains of waters. And God will wipe away every tear from their eyes. (Revelation 7:17)

⁴ And God will wipe away every tear from their eyes; there shall be no more death, nor sorrow, nor crying. There shall be no more pain, for the former things have passed away.

(Revelation 21:4)

¹⁰ And the ransomed of the LORD shall return, and come to Zion with singing,

*with everlasting joy on their heads.
They shall obtain joy and gladness, and
sorrow and sighing shall flee away.*
                                            (Isaiah 35:10)

Glory to God, heaven is a real place! We will really be going there. And, we will not be vapors of smoke floating on a cloud when we go to heaven.

One of the wonderful things about heaven is that our tears and sorrows will be replaced with eternal joy, as promised in the Word of God. Yet, there is much more!

Two

The Throne of God

Heaven is a real place. It is a literal destination. It is not some ephemeral dream, some imagined vision. God has revealed to all of us many of the realities of heaven through the Holy Scriptures.

THE FIRST HEAVEN

First, there is an atmospheric heaven. This is the atmosphere around the earth. It is where the birds fly and the winds blow. This is where showers, storms, mists, vapors, and clouds are formed.

The sky is the place the angel was referring to in Acts 1:11 when he asked the disciples why they were *"gazing up into heaven."* Jesus, when He was talking to His Father, *"lifted up His eyes to heaven"* (John 17:1), or toward the sky.

THE SECOND HEAVEN

Then, there is the heaven of space. This is the region of the sun, the moon, and the stars. It is mentioned in the Bible in many places, a few of which are given here:

> [17] *Blessing I will bless you, and multiplying I will multiply your descendants as the stars of the heaven and as the sand which is on the seashore.*
> (Genesis 22:17)

> [19] *And take heed, lest you lift your eyes to heaven, and when you see the sun, the moon, and the stars, all the host of heaven, you feel driven to worship them and serve them, which the LORD your God has given to all the peoples under the whole heaven as a heritage.*
> (Deuteronomy 4:19)

³¹ *Can you bind the cluster of the Pleiades, or loose the belt of Orion?* ³² *Can you bring out Mazzaroth in its season? Or can you guide the Great Bear with its cubs?* ³³ *Do you know the ordinances of the heavens? Can you set their dominion over the earth?* (Job 38:31–33)

¹⁰ *For the stars of heaven and their constellations will not give their light; the sun will be darkened in its going forth, and the moon will not cause its light to shine.* (Isaiah 13:10)

²⁹ *Immediately after the tribulation of those days the sun will be darkened, and the moon will not give its light; the stars will fall from heaven, and the powers of the heavens will be shaken.* (Matthew 24:29)

THE THIRD HEAVEN

The destination of the righteous, however, is beyond the atmosphere and the starry skies. This place is what the apostle Paul referred to when he wrote, *"I know a man in Christ who fourteen years ago was caught up to the third heaven"* (2 Corinthians 12:2 NIV).

Heaven, as I am using the term throughout this book, is the region often spoken of as the immediate presence of God:

> [24] *For Christ has not entered the holy places made with hands, which are copies of the true, but into heaven itself, now to appear in the presence of God for us.* (Hebrews 9:24)

Heaven is where God lives. When Jesus taught us to pray, He said to pray to *"our Father in heaven"* (Matthew 6:9).

In 1 Kings 8:30, heaven is called the dwelling place of God. In Psalm 11:4, it is called God's holy temple and the place where His throne is.

There, in the temple of God's divine majesty, His excellent glory is revealed in the most conspicuous manner. It is a sacred place of light, joy, and glory. We don't know exactly where the location is, but often in the Bible heaven is indicated as being "up."

We know that God Almighty is in heaven. There He and Jesus Christ are the central focus of saints, angels, and all worshipping beings.

What glorious company there is in heaven! Angels are there, because Jesus said, *"In heaven ...angels always see the face of My Father who is in heaven"* (Matthew 18:10).

The saints are there because Jesus promised us, *"Where I am, there you may be also"* (John 14:3). We are told in 1 Peter 1:4 that an inheritance has been reserved for us in heaven— an inheritance that is incorruptible, undefiled, and that will not fade away.

Saints, it excites me to testify of my beautiful visit to heaven. I am thrilled to tell you of the things I saw and the people I saw.

THE PRAISE OF HEAVEN

After the angel of God had shown me the room of tears, he repeated the litany I heard so often throughout my visits to heaven: "Come and see the glory of your God!"

The radiant, magnificent, celestial splendor of heaven overwhelmed me. The blazes of glory that seemed to shoot from everything I saw filled me with awe. The beauty and bliss of that fair land cannot accurately be pictured by the mind's eye unless a person has seen it for himself.

At that moment, I thought of the words I once heard someone quote:

> The light of heaven
>   Is the face of Jesus.
> The joy of heaven
>   Is the presence of Jesus.
> The harmony of heaven
>   Is the praise of Jesus.
> The theme of heaven
>   Is the work of Jesus.
> The employment of heaven
>   Is the service of Jesus.
> The fullness of heaven
>   Is Jesus Himself.

As I went with the angel, I could feel joy, peace, and happiness everywhere. My thoughts went to my family on earth, and it seemed the angel knew my thoughts. He said to me, "You have a mission to fulfill for God. You are to tell the people on earth what is up here. God is showing you some of heaven, but not all of it. Come and see the glory of your God."

When we reached our destination, I could hear many, many voices singing praises to God.

The magnificent music of the worshippers of heaven thrilled my soul. Honor and glory echoed and reechoed across the wide expanse of heaven as seraphim and saints sang endless anthems of praise with exuberance.

APPROACHING THE THRONE

My soul was exhilarated and transported with joy. Somehow I knew we were nearing the throne of God.

The angel who guided me stopped a long way off, far back from the throne of God. I could see a panoramic view of events that were taking place. I saw the same scene that John saw in his vision that he described in Revelation:

> 11 *Then I looked, and I heard the voice of many angels around the throne, the living creatures, and the elders; and the number of them was ten thousand times ten thousand, and thousands of thousands.* (Revelation 5:11)

Oh, people of earth, if you can only realize what God has in store for us who love Him!

As I gazed in rapture at the scene before me, something even more wonderful happened. I could hear louder than ever these thousands upon thousands of voices praising God. Then— wonder of all wonders!—the angel permitted me to see what I had always longed to see, the throne of God.

THE GLORIOUS THRONE OF GOD

God's throne was *"high and lifted up"* (Isaiah 6:1). Coming out from under the base, the River of Life flowed in its beauty and purity. The glory of God overshadowed the throne. It seemed that lightning, thunder, and voices were all around the throne. John, in describing a vision he had of heaven, said,

> [5] *And from the throne proceeded lightnings, thunderings, and voices. Seven lamps of fire were burning before the throne, which are the seven Spirits of God.* (Revelation 4:5)

I saw a rainbow arching above and around the throne, *"in appearance like an emerald"* (Revelation 4:3). The brilliant, glorious hues of the rainbow were mixed with light, producing dazzlingly intense colors.

It was unlike anything I have ever seen on earth. Varied colors of radiant light signified glory and power. Blazes of splendor flashed from the throne. Beams of glory radiated from it. So much of heaven seems transparent, and those illustrious beams that come forth from the throne are filled with light that is reflected in every part of paradise!

How long I stayed in this heavenly arena, I do not know, but I was overwhelmed with awe. I thought of the thousands who have gone on to heaven and of the many thousands who will yet come. I thought of the holiness of God, the purity of His majesty, and the perfection of His Word. I shouted aloud, "Oh, God! How wonderful it is to behold Your glory and Your majesty and Your power!"

As before, the angel of the Lord said to me, "Come with me. There are many other things in heaven that I want to show you."

THE ROOM OF RECORDS

I was amazed to see a room of records in which meticulous records were being kept. The angel said that God has His angels keep records of every church service on earth and every service in a home where He is lifted up and praised.

God also keeps records on those who are out of His will. He showed me how God's angels keep records of the money that is given in church services, along with a record of the attitudes with which people contribute. He told me of people who have money but won't give to the work of the Lord.

I thought of how Jesus carefully watched the offering and the treasury when He went to the temple of the Lord:

> 41 *Now Jesus sat opposite the treasury and saw how the people put money into the treasury. And many who were rich put in much.*
> 42 *Then one poor widow came and threw in two mites, which make a quadrans* [less than a penny].
> 43 *So He called His disciples to Himself and said to them, "Assuredly, I say to you that this poor widow has put in more than all those who have given to the treasury;*
> 44 *"for they all put in out of their*

abundance, but she out of her poverty put in all that she had, her whole livelihood. "   (Mark 12:41–44)

As the many things were revealed to me, including the room where the record books are kept, the angel reminded me that I was to remember to make a record of these things. He said there were many things that were mysteries to me, as I was only seeing dimly (1 Corinthians 13:12). But the angel emphasized that I was to tell the people on earth about the things I saw.

As we reached another part of heaven, I looked down a very long corridor. Its walls were high, and they seemed to be made of platinum. I could hear the high praises of God ringing out continually. I was amazed at the brilliancy of light and glory that reflected from the walls. Puzzled, I asked, "What is this?" It seemed like the walls were miles long; I couldn't see the end of them.

THE STOREHOUSE OF GOD

The angel who was showing me these things said, "Look at the top of this wall." There on the top of it was etched the word, *Storehouse.*

When I asked, "What are these rooms?" the angel told me these rooms contained blessings that are stored up for God's people!

Heaven is perfect purity, and God wants to purify His saints on earth so they will enjoy heaven's atmosphere. Heaven is fullness of joy, and God desires to give joy to His people on earth. Heaven is everlasting freedom, and God longs for His people to have deliverance while on earth. Heaven is perfect wholeness, and God wants to heal His people here on earth. Heaven is complete security, and God wants His people to feel confident and secure here on earth. Heaven is fruition and fulfillment, and God desires that His people be fulfilled on earth.

When Jesus instructed us to pray that God's *"will be done on earth as it is in heaven"* (Matthew 6:10), He revealed that God wants us to have a taste of heaven here on earth!

Saints, the Lord has storehouses of blessings just for you. They are waiting in heaven for you to claim them and to receive them now, here on earth. God wants to save you. He wants to deliver you. He wants to heal you. He wants you to know *the peace of God, which surpasses all understanding"* (Philippians 4:7). He wants you to experience a lasting *"joy inexpressible and full of glory"* (1 Peter 1:8).

THE HEALING JESUS

"See the glory of your God," the angel proclaimed. When he disappeared, Jesus stood beside me.

I looked at Jesus. He seemed to be taller now than I had perceived Him to be before. The brilliant robe He wore hung on Him elegantly and gracefully. Sandals graced His scarred feet, and His face and hair were glorious and beautiful.

As I gazed at Him, I asked, "Jesus, what are these rooms?"

The Lord didn't speak to me, but He put out His hand and moved it toward the wall. At that moment, a large opening appeared in the wall. All around the edges of the opening I saw glory and power and light. Like every other object, this seemed to give glory to God.

I cried out, "Oh, Lord, what is this?"

He said to me, "My child, these are for My people. They are for sinners on the earth, if they will only believe. I died to make them whole."

As I looked into His eyes, I knew that He wanted people to believe that He, Jesus Christ, had died so that we could be made whole. He said, "Healings are waiting for people on earth. The day will come when there will be an avalanche of miracles and healings on the earth."

Continuing, He said, "Child, as far as you can see, these are supply buildings, or storehouses. The blessings contained here await the belief of those on earth. All they have to do is believe and receive—believe that I am the Lord Jesus Christ and that I am able to do these things, and receive My gifts."

"When you go back to the earth," He emphasized, "remember that it is not you who does the healing. It is not the vessel that heals; it is I. Just speak my Word and pray, and I will do the healing. Believe that I can do it."

I shouted, "Glory to God! Hallelujah! Thank You, Jesus!"

Jesus put His hand down, and the opening in the wall closed.

Then the angel and I traveled at a very fast speed to another place. Here, too, I could hear the music and the glorious shouts of the people of God. The angel said, "Child, I've been commanded by the Lord to show you several things. Tell the people about these things."

Three

Before, Now, and After

A t this point in my vision, the angel of the Lord began to reveal things to me that I had often wondered about previously. He began to tell me about a great mystery.

He said, "God has spoken, and I am to show you before, now, and after. The things I am going to show will give you great excitement. I am going to reveal to you what happens when a person is born again. I will show you how a person's sins are washed away by the blood of the Lamb in the record rooms.

"I am going to show you what happens when a born-again individual dies on earth and his soul comes to heaven. Come and see the glory of your God."

We traveled from heaven at a fast rate of speed, and soon we were back over the earth. I could see the earth as in a vision, and the angel said to me, "Look and behold."

As the angel allowed the vision to pass before me, I saw a beautiful little church in the country. Now, I don't know where the church was located geographically, but it was a rural church, way out in the country.

With the assistance of the angel of God, I was allowed to look into the building. I could see about thirty people seated in the pews. The pastor in the pulpit preached on this passage:

> [6] *Seek the LORD while He may be found.*
> *Call upon Him while He is near.*
> [7] *Let the wicked forsake his way, and the*
> *unrighteous man his thoughts; let him*

*return to the LORD, and He will have
mercy on him; and to our God, for He
will abundantly pardon.* (Isaiah 55:6–7)

As I gazed on this scene, I saw a mighty
angel standing over the church. The guiding angel beside me said, "A large angel is stationed at
every church. This angel is in charge of all the
other angels of that church."

ANGELS AT CHURCH

Two angels with books stood outside the
door of the church. I could see people going in
and out of the church. Then my angel guide sig-
naled with his hand, and it seemed as if the roof
rolled back, and I could see inside the church.

An angel stood on each side of the pastor at
the pulpit. Beyond those two were two more angels. This made four angels around the pulpit.

Two angels stood at the back of the church,
behind the congregation. Two more stood about
halfway up the aisle, and up near the altar stood
two more angels. So there were quite a few angels in the church, and several of them had
scrolls and pens in their hands.

The angel said to me, "I want to show you what happens."

The pastor began to speak, and the ushers started to take up the offering. As the offering was received, the angels recorded the people's attitudes in giving. They recorded the contributors' thoughts—whether they begrudged giving to the work of the Lord, or if they enjoyed giving the offering and viewed it as an act of worship. The angels logged it all in their record books.

Then the two big angels in the front of the pulpit nodded their heads at the other angels.

These activities of the angels were invisible to the people in the church, but I could see it all clearly. Then my guide said to me, "I want to show you something else. Watch closely, and you will be blessed."

Suddenly, it seemed as if I had been moved behind the pastor. As he was preaching on the sixth verse—*"Seek the LORD while He may be found. Call upon Him while He is near"*—I could see a host of heavenly beings inside the church. All the time the service was going on, the angels were rejoicing.

The minister was anointed as he preached that message. One of the angels was pouring what looked like fire on his head. The glories of God were coming from the preacher's mouth.

At the back of the church, a door opened, and a man who was very drunk staggered in. He came down the aisle, saying, "I am the one you are talking to, preacher. I need the Lord. I need to be saved. I am an alcoholic." The man dropped to his knees at the front altar and began to cry out to God.

Two of the deacons went to the altar to minister to him. Putting their arms around him, they asked him, "Do you mean business with God? Do you really want to be saved?"

"Yes, I want to be saved," the man said. "I'm an alcoholic. I need to be set free."

A SOUL IS SAVED

Two more angels suddenly appeared. They had scrolls in their hands, and they began to write down what the man said. Then the deacons began to lead him through the process of salvation.

I saw that this man was filled with sin. However, as the deacons prayed with him, one of the angels touched his heart, and smoke as dark as a rain cloud came spewing out of his chest.

When I saw this, I recalled some of the Scriptures that talk about the vile sins that come out of the heart:

> [35] *A good man out of the good treasure of his heart brings forth good things, and an evil man out of the evil treasure brings forth evil things.*
>
> (Matthew 12:35)

> [18] *But the things that come out of the mouth come from the heart, and these make a man "unclean."*
> [19] *For out of the heart come evil thoughts, murder, adultery, sexual immorality, theft, false testimony, slander.*
>
> (Matthew 15:18–19 NIV)

As the man began to pray to God with upraised hands, I saw wide, black bands that were wrapped all around him. He was in bondage to all kinds of sin, but especially to alcohol addiction and drunkenness. A deacon said to him, "You must confess these sins to God, so that He can forgive you, and so you can be washed in the blood of the Lamb."

As he began to confess his sins, an angel touched him. I could see fire come from the angel's hands. The bands started to break and burst off of him.

This gave the man tremendous liberty. He raised his hands and praised the Lord. He stood up, and I saw the glory of God come down on him. I know the Lord sobered him up, because he began to shout praises to the Lord.

Then the two mighty angels looked at each other and nodded their heads. They came back through the air to where we were and said, "Come and see the glory of God."

IN THE RECORD ROOMS AGAIN

We traveled back to heaven with the other two angels very rapidly. After we entered through the gate, we went down a beautiful pathway that appeared to be made of gold. Quickly we were transported to a lovely room.

The angel said, "Come and see what we do here."

The long corridor we were in led to many other rooms similar to the one we were entering. The angel said, "There are many of these rooms in heaven. These are called rooms of records. You will see what goes on in these rooms."

The angel said, "We are going to the room that contains the name of the man who was just converted on earth."

In the room I saw the angels from earth go quickly and give the report written on a scroll to another angel.

Several ladders were positioned along the walls in the rectangular room. Shelves covered the walls, and all the books were on the shelves. The scene reminded me of a library on earth.

Other angels, singing and praising God, stood in a line in front of a large desk. It was about eight feet across and four feet wide. A square cutout was in the center of the desk, which was overlaid with solid gold. It was so beautiful. It was carved with leaves and fruit.

It was the most beautiful desk one could ever imagine. I have never seen anything like it—or even a picture like it—on the earth. I was caught up with the glory and the majesty of God in this room.

Angels were going up and down ladders. They were continuously pulling books down from the shelves and returning them to the correct places. Several angels were standing nearby with reports from other parts of the earth.

I noticed that some of the books in the wall were different shades of color. Then I saw two of the angels from the church standing in a line with a book they had pulled from the shelf. It contained the record of the very man I had just witnessed being born again on earth.

The angel with me said, "Do you see the two angels from the church service?"

"Yes."

"Do you see the book in their hands?"

"Yes."

"That is the record book of the man who just got saved. They have retrieved it from the shelves. Now they must go to the angel in charge."

My guide explained that in every record room, there is an angel in charge. Everything that goes in or out of the room goes past that angel. All is done in order to the glory of God.

I was amazed to see all these things going on. The angel in charge wore a brilliant headdress that is beyond my capacity to describe. He had golden hair and a glistening, white robe with a lot of gold on it. This gorgeous angel had a wingspread of about twelve feet. He was the most beautiful angel I had ever seen. The angel was the main recordkeeper of that room.

The angel in charge looked at me and motioned for me to come to his side. The power of God moved me, and I was quickly standing by the angel's right side.

He said to me, "You are allowed to be here so that we can show you what happens when someone on earth is born again. You are to tell the people on earth."

The wonder of it thrilled me beyond words!

KEEPING RECORDS

As I looked out in front of me, the high praises of God were going up all around. I could hear bells ringing, although I could not see them. Delightful, laughing, glorious, happy angels stood with books in their hands, waiting to talk to the angel in charge.

I started to praise and magnify God anew for His wondrous power and His glorious acts.

"Do you see the two angels in front of the desk?" my angel guide asked me.

"Yes," I replied.

"They were present when this man was born again."

He pulled a message out of the scroll; it was like a marker in the book. I couldn't see what was written on the paper or the scroll. Then the angel said, "Look at what is written here," as he showed it to me.

The message was written in an orderly fashion, and it was beautiful. I saw the name of the country, the name of the state, the name of the county, the name of the city, and the name of the church.

The angel showed me the name of the pastor and how many people were in the church. He showed me the order of the service. The entire record was written down. He showed me the people who participated in the church service and the details of the offering that was taken.

The name of the man whose salvation I had seen on earth was recorded on the paper. The message of the Gospel of the Lord Jesus Christ that was preached to save his soul and the exact time to the very second he was born again—it was all written there. I shouted, "Glory to God!"

When the written account got to the point where the man prayed the sinner's prayer and received Jesus Christ as Lord and Savior, the angel looked at the two messenger angels and asked, "Were you witnesses that this man was born again at this hour and this time?"

They said, "Yes, we were witnesses. We were there. He received Jesus Christ as Lord and Savior. We saw it happen."

The noise of the glory, the praises, and the shouts that went up at that moment was astounding. All of heaven was magnifying God.

Then the angel wrote something in the book he kept and closed the pages. The book was very thick. He said to me, "Look behind you."

I saw many people, redeemed saints, dressed in white robes and arrayed in splendor.

THE BLOOD OF JESUS

These redeemed saints of the Most High God were singing this song:

> Oh, nothing but the blood of Jesus
> Can wash my sins away.
> Oh, nothing but the blood of Jesus
> Can make me whole today.
> Oh, nothing but the blood of Jesus
> Can cleanse me today.
> I've been redeemed
> By the blood of the Lamb.

As I observed, the man's book was handed to one of the rejoicing saints. Page after page of the old writings were washed away. They lifted up the pages one by one, and I could see that every page had been washed in the blood of Jesus. Nothing of this person's sins remained. And this Scripture came to me from Isaiah:

> *25 I, even I, am he who blots out your transgressions, for my own sake, and remembers your sins no more.*
>
> (Isaiah 43:25)

I thought, "Oh, God, how beautiful it is that Your Word still marches on. That man's sins were washed away by the blood of the Lamb."

As I watched, the book was handed to another angel. This heavenly being had long, beautiful hair. The book was laid on a tray that the angel carried. The angels saluted each other, and shouts of glory went up.

The angel who accompanied me said, "Come and see the glory of your God." I began traveling with him at a very fast pace through the corridors of heaven.

THE LAMB'S BOOK OF LIFE

Again I stood before the throne of God. Dear ones, there were horns blowing, and the sound of trumpets blared. A cloud of glory, the Shekinah glory, illuminated the entire area around the throne.

There was much thunder and lightning. I could hear a multitude of voices saying, "Glory to God! Hallelujah!"

I watched this mighty scene, and I saw the angel lay the book on the altar of God and bow down low. The voice of God resonated loudly through the air, yet I understood every word. God said, "Another soul has been redeemed by My Son's blood. Another person has received eternal salvation through the blood of My Son."

All the bells of heaven were ringing! All of heaven's populace was shouting! I bowed down and began to praise God.

I saw the Lamb's Book of Life (Revelation 21:27) on the altar of God, and I saw a hand come out of that cloud and open up the book that was laid there by the angel. Then the man's name was written down in the Lamb's Book of Life. Glory to God! Saints, our names are surely written down in the Book of Life, also.

As I watched this mighty scene, the angel of God said, "Come and see the glory of God." Immediately, I was taken out of heaven again at the speed of light. As I went with the angel, I thought of this passage from Isaiah:

> [3] *I will give you the treasures of darkness and hidden riches of secret places, that you may know that I, the LORD, who call you by your name, am the God of Israel.*

> [4] *For Jacob My servant's sake, and Israel My elect, I have even called you by your name; I have named you, though you have not known Me.* (Isaiah 45:3–4)

RIVER OF LIFE

In the next scene of my vision, I watched as the Lord took the saints of the living God through the River of Life. Oh, the River of Life flows from the throne of God and the Lamb (Revelation 22:1). As the saints passed through the River of Life, I could hear them shouting, "Glory to God!"

Then I saw a countless company of saints who were being clothed in the whitest, most gorgeous robes anyone could ever see. I remembered that John wrote this:

> [13] *Then one of the elders answered, saying to me, "Who are these arrayed in white robes, and where did they come from?"* [14] *And I said to him, "Sir, you know." So he said to me, "These are the ones who come out of the great tribulation, and washed their robes and made them white in the blood of the Lamb."*
> (Revelation 7:13–14)

BEFORE THE THRONE

I was allowed to go again before the throne of God and witness an awesome, exciting scene. I could hear the sound of trumpets as I stood before the throne of God. Words fail me to describe adequately the thrill and awe I felt.

Twelve angels stood ministering before the throne, arrayed in garments beyond any worthy description. The best I can tell you is that on the breastplates of their apparel, they had jewels embedded in their garments. Atop their heads they had some kind of heavenly material of glorious colors. Gold edging adorned their long robes.

The blare of trumpets announced the saints as they came, one by one, to stand before God. An inestimable number of saints, angels, and heavenly beings made up a huge gallery. All of them were glorifying God.

REDEEMED ONES

The redeemed of all ages were glorious and beautiful. They were real people—not puffs of smoke or clouds floating in space.

75

Everywhere I looked, I saw the angels of God praising His majesty continuously.

Standing before the throne, I heard a great voice saying:

> [3] *Behold, the tabernacle of God is with men, and He will dwell with them, and they shall be His people. God Himself will be with them and be their God.*
>
> (Revelation 21:3)

Then I saw a cloud of glory filled with lightning, thunder, and voices. As I looked, I saw the hand of God come out of the cloud and begin to wipe the tears of the saints from their eyes. The Word says that *"God will wipe away every tear from their eyes"* (Revelation 21:4).

I heard God say,

> [4] *There shall be no more death, nor sorrow, nor crying. There shall be no more pain, for the former things have passed away.*
> [5] *...Behold, I make all things new.*
>
> (Revelation 21:4–5)

God said to the assembled saints, "I see that your names are written in the Lamb's Book of Life. Welcome into the joy of the Lord."

Once again, another Scripture came to my mind:

> [21] *Well done, good and faithful servant; you were faithful over a few things, I will make you ruler over many things. Enter into the joy of your lord.*
>
> (Matthew 25:21)

With that the Lord placed magnificent golden crowns on the heads of all of His sanctified ones.

I knew that the blessings of God would continue to flow for all of the redeemed. I knew they would never end!

Four

Storehouses of Heaven

I believe Jesus Christ revealed heaven to me as He did in order to give me balance. He knew that I had been through many visits to hell, and experiencing hell was so horrible that He gave me the blessing of seeing heaven.

On one of my visits to heaven, I was shown God's storehouses. The angel of the Lord said to me, "Come and see the glory of your God."

The angel was very beautiful and tall. His rainbow-colored wings were shaped like triangles. He told me that God had given him instructions, and he was to show me parts of heaven.

We began to go up higher through the atmosphere and went through the entrance to heaven again. I saw fruit trees loaded with beautiful fruit. I saw families dressed in beautiful robes, walking up and down the hillside, praising God.

The environment was saturated with the most beautiful music you would ever want to hear. Heavenly music is a manifestation of joy. It is an evidence of happiness, a proof of joy.

I have heard magnificent choirs and grand ensembles that created and performed beautiful music here on earth. But, saints, nothing down here can compare with the splendor and beauty of the music and singing there.

Heaven was a symphony of music. Imagine, if you can, millions of perfectly pitched voices, sweetly singing the melodies of heaven! Not a single one was off-key. Everything was in perfect harmony.

Stringed instruments provided beautiful accompaniment, along with trumpets and other kinds of musical instruments. They all blended with the voices of the redeemed saints who were praising God with rapturous joy. The tones of the instruments, like the singing voices, had been purified and made perfect by the power of Almighty God.

Oh, it was glorious to hear the wonderful praises to God. Voices that are without quality of tone or pitch on earth will sing in beautiful harmony in heaven. We will all be happy over there. Even a ten-thousand-voice choir here would pale in comparison with the grand and eloquent music of God's celestial city!

Wave after wave of unbelievable anthems of praise billowed over the landscape and through the streets of heaven. It was so all-encompassing that I could hear or think of nothing else for some time.

Finally, the angel said, "Come and see the glory of God."

I remember going with him through an area that had the greenest grass imaginable.

There were huge clusters of flowers in certain parts of the grass. The flowers were splendid and looked somewhat like roses. Each plant had at least one bloom consisting of beautiful petals. And, saints, the flowers looked like they were singing!

HORSES OF HEAVEN

Traveling on with the angel, we passed a place where there were beautiful, white horses. I remembered reading in Revelation about horses and how Jesus will one day be astride a white horse, leading the armies of heaven, who will also be riding white horses:

> [11] *Now I saw heaven opened, and behold, a white horse. And He who sat on him was called Faithful and True, and in righteousness He judges and makes war.*
> [12] *His eyes were like a flame of fire, and on His head were many crowns. He had a name written that no one knew except Himself.*
> [13] *He was clothed with a robe dipped in blood, and His name is called The Word of God.*

*14 And the armies in heaven, clothed in
fine linen, white and clean, followed
Him on white horses.*

(Revelation 19:11–14)

These horses looked as noble as marble
chess pieces. They looked as if they were huge
statues that had been chiseled out of boulders,
but they were real and alive. Their hooves were
gigantic. They were pure white and very regal.

A woman dressed in a beautiful robe was
smiling and talking to the horses, directing them
to bow their knees in praise to God. All of them,
at the same time, bowed their right knees and
praised the Lord!

I thought, "Oh, how beautiful!" And I remembered reading in the Bible that every creature in heaven and on earth would honor and
praise God:

*23 I have sworn by Myself; the word has
gone out of My mouth in righteousness,
and shall not return, that to Me every
knee shall bow, every tongue shall take
an oath.* (Isaiah 45:23)

*11 For it is written: "As I live, says the
LORD, Every knee shall bow to Me, and*

every tongue shall confess to God."

(Romans 14:11)

⁹ Therefore God also has highly exalted Him and given Him the name which is above every name,
¹⁰ that at the name of Jesus every knee should bow, of those in heaven, and of those on earth, and of those under the earth,
¹¹ and that every tongue should confess that Jesus Christ is Lord, to the glory of God the Father. (Philippians 2:9–11)

¹³ Every creature which is in heaven and on the earth and under the earth and such as are in the sea, and all that are in them, I heard saying: "Blessing and honor and glory and power be to Him who sits on the throne, and to the Lamb, forever and ever!" (Revelation 5:13)

Peace, joy, and happiness were everywhere. I could hear people praising God.

Suddenly, I could no longer see the angel with me, but there stood Jesus. He seemed to me to be very tall in stature, and He wore a robe that was distinctive from the robes of others.

His piercing eyes were beautiful. He had what looked like a neatly-trimmed beard and very thick hair. I remember looking at Him and thinking that the tenderness in His eyes is beyond a writer's description. The loveliness of the Blessed Savior was awe-inspiring and wonderful.

Everything within me wanted to praise Him, to worship and bow before Him, the King of Kings and Lord of Lords, Jesus Christ. Glory and power billowed all around Him.

STOREHOUSES OF HEALING

I noticed that Jesus' eyes had taken on a troubled look. I asked, "Jesus, what is it?"

"Child, look!"

He waved His hand toward a building where I saw a large opening. From the opening, glory and power—billows and billows of power—came streaming out.

I asked Him again, "Jesus, what is this?"

"Child, do you see the healings in these storehouses?"

"Yes, Lord."

"All of these blessings await the people of God."

The sufferings in this life are indeed tragic.

How much sickness, disease, physical affliction, deformity, and similar ills people suffer here!

You see it everywhere. Just walk up and down the corridors of any hospital or major medical center. Visit the contagious disease wards, the mental health wings, the intensive care facilities, the emergency rooms, and other places that take care of people in terrible pain and unbearable physical and mental anguish.

Sickness is a result of the fall of Adam and Eve in the Garden of Eden. It is one of sin's consequences. Some see sickness as a nuisance, a tragedy of the human condition, or just a part of normal existence. In reality, it is a curse of Satan.

HEALING IN HEAVEN

The need for healing is overwhelming.

Sickness is a corruption of God's will. It is an unnatural element in the economy of God. It does not originate with God; it does not come from heaven. Sin is from an evil source, not a good source.

When we get to heaven, all sickness, disease, and suffering will be gone forever. Paul wrote of the ultimate redemption of our bodies:

> [18] *For I consider that the sufferings of this present time are not worthy to be compared with the glory which shall be revealed in us.*
> [19] *For the earnest expectation of the creation eagerly waits for the revealing of the sons of God.* (Romans 8:18–19)

The worst physical suffering possible in this life is not worthy of comparison with the exceedingly wonderful glory that will be hereafter. In heaven with perfect bodies, we will rest in Christ with no more pain or physical affliction. Still, He also wants us to be healed now.

One of the names of God in the Bible is *Jehovah-Rapha,* which means "the Lord, our Healer." God made a special covenant of healing with His people. He promised Israel:

> [26] *If you diligently heed the voice of the LORD your God and do what is right in His sight, give ear to His commandments and keep all His statutes, I will put none of the diseases on you which I have brought on the Egyptians. For I am the LORD who heals you.*
> (Exodus 15:26)

Although sickness is part of the curse of sin, Jesus has lifted the curse for believers through His atonement for sin. The wounds and bruises Christ suffered paid the price for sin. He became our Savior. Yet, His suffering did more than just pay for sin: it established and authenticated Jesus as Healer!

> [5] *But He was wounded for our transgressions, He was bruised for our iniquities; the chastisement for our peace was upon Him, and by His stripes we are healed.* (Isaiah 53:5)

> [24] [Jesus] *Himself bore our sins in His own body on the tree, that we, having died to sins, might live for righteousness; by whose stripes you were healed.*
> (1 Peter 2:24)

HEALING IS FOR TODAY

The healing ministry of Christ did not cease when He was taken up from the disciples into heaven. The Acts of the Apostles is a continuation *"of all that Jesus began both to do and teach"* (Acts 1:1).

Jesus modeled a healing ministry on earth

and taught that healing is a part of the kingdom benefits. Before He returned to His Father, Jesus instructed believers to go and heal the sick. He said,

> [17] *And these signs will follow those who believe: In My name they will cast out demons; they will speak with new tongues;*
> [18] *They will take up serpents; and if they drink anything deadly, it will by no means hurt them; they will lay hands on the sick, and they will recover.*
>
> (Mark 16:17–18)

Jesus also told us:

> [13] *And whatever you ask in My name, that I will do, that the Father may be glorified in the Son.*
> [14] *If you ask anything in My name, I will do it.*
> [15] *If you love Me, keep My commandments.* (John 14:13–15)

Christ seemed to have disappeared, and I was walking with the angel among the storehouses. I thought, "So many storehouses, Lord."

Jesus spoke to my spirit: "Child, when you pray for somebody on the earth, pray for them in

My name. Remember that you don't do the healing—I do. Ask Me to heal an eye or leg, and I will do it. Ask Me to straighten crooked limbs or heal sick bodies, and I will heal them.

"Whatever you want Me to do, ask in My name, and I will do it. I have the answers waiting in these storehouses."

Jesus emphasized that the blessings in these storehouses were for His people and for the sinners on the earth. I remembered that He had said that very soon there will be an avalanche of healings in the world.

I thought of the healings that are already occurring on the earth, and I thought, "Lord, how wonderful You are to repair our bodies!"

As we grow older, our bodies begin to wear out or deteriorate. That is a natural effect of sin, and we will never be entirely free from these consequences. But God doesn't desire that we spend our later years bedridden and ineffective. He wants to keep us active and productive. Jesus died so we could be made whole.

Jesus Christ, the Son of God, shed His blood so that we could be saved from hell. If we believe that Jesus Christ is the Son of God, we have hope. The hope for our souls is in Jesus.

Jesus Christ suffered for the healing of our bodies. Our privilege, our blessing, and our hope for wholeness and wellness are in Jesus. He is the hope for our physical well-being.

Saints, there are storehouses of unclaimed blessings in heaven. They are ready to be claimed by God's people who ask in faith—and in the name of Jesus!

When He was on earth, the Lord once said, *"I go* [away] *to prepare a place for you"* (John 14:2). The place He is preparing is in heaven. It is a beautiful place of many beautiful things.

As I give my testimony in this book and as I speak about heaven, the thoughts of that place thrill my soul. Thank God for the beautiful Word that He has given unto us, His children!

Five

Order in Heaven

Heaven is a busy place. It is filled with activity and excitement. Angels are always doing things; they are always engaged in useful, industrious enterprises.

One purpose of this book is to tell you how I saw the angels working in heaven. They are happy and joyful—never tired, never sad. They are always praising God.

Redeemed saints are busy in heaven, too. They always have work to do. Exactly what kind of work all the saints are engaged in, I do not know. But you can be sure that no one is idle in that fair land.

Saints are busy in kinds of work that no one on earth has ever experienced. They are engaged in stimulating, exhilarating, fulfilling tasks. They are continually glorifying God and doing the things God ordained for them to do.

When I saw the angels who flew from the earth with reports, they were coming into heaven from all over the world. They had been to many church services and many prayer meetings.

While observing the things on the earth, they always held in their hands white pieces of paper that looked like scrolls, which had gold edges. Then they would return to certain areas of heaven and share their reports with other angels.

HEAVEN'S POPULATION

In one area of heaven I saw saintly men who wore beautiful, glorious, white robes. Immediately, I thought of this Scripture:

> [10] *I will greatly rejoice in the LORD, my soul shall be joyful in my God; for He has clothed me with the garments of salvation, He has covered me with the robe of righteousness, as a bridegroom decks himself with ornaments, and as a bride adorns herself with her jewels.*
>
> (Isaiah 61:10)

The people I saw in heaven had distinctive features and were from all nations of the earth. The Holy Scriptures say:

> [9] *After these things I looked, and behold, a great multitude which no one could number, of all nations, tribes, peoples, and tongues, standing before the throne and before the Lamb, clothed with white robes, with palm branches in their hands.* (Revelation 7:9)

Another thing that made a lasting impression on me was the fact that heaven is such an orderly place. Everything that was done was always done thoroughly, properly, and with the highest degree of excellence. No work was shoddy; no product poor; no activity mediocre.

When I saw families walking on the holy hills of heaven and praising God, it was such a beautiful sight. Their joy and happiness were uninhibited and without restraint. They seemed to be always going and doing marvelous deeds in the Lord's presence.

Everything, whether done individually or in groups, was done in an orderly fashion. Heaven is completely free of impurities and imperfections. It is perfect in every sense of the word. All of the alterations and changes we are familiar with here on earth are unknown in the paradise of God. Perfect joy and peace fill the hearts, souls, and bodies of all who are there.

PERFECT ORDER

Divine, perfect order and purpose characterize everything that happens in heaven.

Both angels and saints are continuously engaged in excellent, joyful service. No one is idle. No one is ever bored. God's children, as well as the angels and all the heavenly creatures, serve Him day and night forever.

When we receive new heavenly bodies after the resurrection of the saints, we will never grow tired or become weak. We will never know fatigue. Our supernatural, glorified bodies will never lose their strength. In eternity, time is suspended and circumstances do not ravage the mind, the will, or the body.

To engage in the employments and enjoyments of heaven, we must have a heavenly nature. And this is what happens when we are born again—we become *"partakers of the divine nature"* (2 Peter 1:4), as Peter explained:

> ³ *His divine power has given us everything we need for life and godliness through our knowledge of him who called us by his own glory and goodness.* ⁴ *Through these he has given us his very great and precious promises, so that through them you may participate in the divine nature and escape the corruption in the world caused by evil desires.*
>
> (2 Peter 1:3–4 NIV)

The architecture of heaven was designed and built in eternity past by the eternal God. In one part I saw what looked like an entire block of the city of heaven. The buildings were very large, and across the top of each was a huge, impressive crown made of many jewels.

I don't know how many people occupied those grand buildings because I didn't go inside any of them. But they were all stately and spacious, far beyond anything you have ever seen on earth.

I thought of how the Scriptures say that when we are laboring on earth for Jesus, we are laying up treasures in heaven (Luke 18:22). I remembered these verses:

> 16 *And the twenty-four elders who sat before God on their thrones fell on their faces and worshiped God,*
> 17 *saying: "We give You thanks, O Lord God Almighty, the One who is and who was and who is to come, because You have taken Your great power and reigned.*
> 18 *"The nations were angry, and Your wrath has come, and the time of the dead, that they should be judged, and that You should reward Your servants the prophets and the saints, and those who fear Your name, small and great, and should destroy those who destroy the earth."*   (Revelation 11:16–18)
>
> 23 *For indeed your reward is great in heaven.*   (Luke 6:23)

¹² *And behold, I* [Jesus] *am coming quickly, and My reward is with Me, to give to every one according to his work.*
(Revelation 22:12)

CHARIOTS OF GOD

As we moved to another part of heaven, the angel of the Lord said to me, "Come and see the glory of your God."

The angel showed me the chariots of God. The wheels of them were so large they are difficult to describe. They were studded with diamonds and precious rubies and emeralds.

Each chariot had at least two wheels on each side. The fronts of the chariots were low and open like sleighs. They seemed as if they were on fire, but they were never consumed.

BODIES OF QUALITY

The features of all the people I saw in heaven were glorified and beautiful. Not one person had any scars, and they all looked radiant and handsome.

I have heard people say, "Well, we are just going to be a vapor of smoke." No, you are not going to be a vapor of smoke. You will have a bodily form and features.

The Bible says there are elders around the throne:

> 4 *Around the throne were twenty-four thrones, and on the thrones I saw twenty-four elders sitting, clothed in white robes; and they had crowns of gold on their heads.* (Revelation 4:4)

The patriarchs in heaven are beautiful saints of God who have died and gone on before us. God has given them eternal life. I saw them as they will be when they receive their new, glorified bodies after the Resurrection.

Saints, you will be unbelievably happy in heaven. When I was in heaven, memories of home were far away. There was no sadness there, no sorrow, no grief. I was delighted in the joy of the Lord and awed by His beauty.

There was no darkness in heaven. There was only glory and might and power everywhere, especially as you neared the throne. The River of Life flowed from beneath the throne; it was beautiful and looked like a sea of glass:

¹ And he showed me a pure river of water of life, clear as crystal, proceeding from the throne of God and of the Lamb. (Revelation 22:1)

As I was going, the angel said, "Come and see the glory of God."

Saints, I was taken at a very fast pace by the angel to a place where the high praises of God and the music seemed to grow in intensity and volume. It was the most beautiful music you would ever want to hear. Sounds of joy and shouting were everywhere.

The angel of the Lord said, "We are approaching the throne." I thought, "Oh, God, how glorious, how beautiful!"

WHEN GOD SPEAKS

When God speaks, it seems that twelve very large angels, each of them twelve to fifteen feet tall, stand in front of the throne. How they blow their trumpets!

Beautiful jewels adorn the fronts of their garments. With music and with all of the things they say and do, they influence the atmosphere.

They seem to prepare the way for the Lord to speak.

I could see a thick cloud enveloping the mighty throne when the Lord spoke or proclaimed a message.

> [5] *And from the throne proceeded lightnings, thunderings, and voices. Seven lamps of fire were burning before the throne, which are the seven Spirits of God.* (Revelation 4:5)

Then power would billow out from the front of the throne. In the midst of the throne, God Almighty dwells in a cloud of glory.

When God spoke, His voice sounded *"like many waters"* (Revelation 14:2), but I understood every word of it. Once God began to speak about His Son's blood. He spoke of how His Son's blood was shed for all people in the earth. He said that the blood of Jesus Christ His Son can cleanse us from all sin (1 John 1:7), and He extended this invitation:

> [17] *Whoever is thirsty, let him come; and whoever wishes, let him take the free gift of the water of life.* (Revelation 22:17 NIV)

God said that His Son's blood was shed to redeem men and women from their sins. He said that putting His Son on the cross to give us eternal life was worth everything, and that His Son's blood had paid the price to redeem us.

> ⁷ *In Him we have redemption through His blood, the forgiveness of sins, according to the riches of His grace.*
>
> (Ephesians 1:7)

> ¹⁴ *In whom we have redemption through His blood, the forgiveness of sins.*
>
> (Colossians 1:14)

> ⁵ *Jesus Christ...loved us and washed us from our sins in His own blood.*
>
> (Revelation 1:5)

When I was in heaven, it was so a thrilling and exciting to hear the voice of God. Although it was a mighty roar, the voice of God was pleasant. I could understand everything He said.

I kept thinking, "Oh, God, how beautiful You are! You prepared all things. You made all things for us, Lord! We cannot even begin to think of the things that You prepared for us who love You" (1 Corinthians 2:9).

HEAVEN, A REAL PLACE

I remember thinking, "Heaven is real. These people are real. These angels are real. All of this is beautiful and real, and someday I am going to inherit this as I continue to serve the Lord."

Talking about heaven and the splendor of God is a joy to me. I thank Him with all of my heart for being able to serve Him. I thank God that Jesus Christ saved my soul from a wretched hell. I thank God that I am a born-again, blood-washed child of the King and that Jesus Christ is my Lord!

If you are not born again, you need to be saved from your sins. You need to ask Jesus Christ to come into your heart and save your soul.

Believe that He is the Son of God. Believe that God the Father sent Him to this earth, that He was born of Mary, a virgin, and that He is the holy Son of God, sent to redeem us from hell. Most of all, you need to believe that Jesus paid the only acceptable sacrifice for your sins when He died on the cross.

Six

What Happens to Children

I n biblical days Jesus spoke about the little children. He said, *"Let the little children come to Me, and do not forbid them; for of such is the kingdom of heaven"* (Matthew 19:14).

Jesus also said these things:

> [3] *Assuredly, I say to you, unless you are converted and become as little children, you will by no means enter the kingdom of heaven.*

⁴ Therefore whoever humbles himself as this little child is the greatest in the kingdom of heaven. (Matthew 18:3–4)

¹⁵ Assuredly, I say to you, whoever does not receive the kingdom of God as a little child will by no means enter it.
(Mark 10:15)

³⁷ Whoever receives one of these little children in My name receives Me; and whoever receives Me, receives not Me but Him who sent Me. (Mark 9:37)

Also, in the Old Testament it says,

¹ Tell your children about it, let your children tell their children, and their children another generation. (Joel 1:3)

This part of heaven is really going to thrill many people. Many people have criticized this, but I know that God showed it to me. It happened during one of my trips into heaven.

I was with the great angel with mighty rainbow-colored, triangle-shaped wings. The angel wore a white, glistening garment, and his hair was like spun gold. His features were beautiful and glorious. Light and power were all over him.

He said, "Come and see the glory of God. God has said that I must show you the place where children go and what happens to them when they die."

I want to clear up something right now. When the Lord Jesus showed me hell, I did not see any children at all. There were no little children or infants in hell that I can remember.

This may not agree with the theories of other people, but I am going to tell you what the angel of the Lord showed me about heaven and hell and the place where children go.

I was just praising God and traveling with the angel. We were high in the atmosphere when we stopped and the angel said, "I must show you these things."

REMEMBERING

When I was with the angel of the Lord, many things occurred that I do not remember now. I was not allowed to remember some of them. There were many events that happened on my trip to heaven—things I was shown but cannot recall. However, what I am permitted to remember is enough to motivate me to tell you about heaven!

Daniel had complete understanding of all of his visions and dreams. However, when the Lord took me into heaven—oh, my—there was such glory and power! Things were going on that were not explained to me, and I was only taken into certain parts of heaven. To me the most wonderful part was for babies and little children.

UNBORN BABIES

When the angel of God said, "Come and see," he moved his hand in the air, and a vision of a hospital appeared. I saw a woman in the labor room, having a child.

The angel of the Lord said to me, "She is having a miscarriage. The baby is only three months old."

As I took in the scene, two beautiful angels appeared by her bed. In their hands they held what looked like a basket made of white marble and pearl. It was the most beautiful thing I have ever seen. It opened up in the center and closed on each side.

The angels were praising God. I could hear them. When the woman had the miscarriage, the baby's spirit, like a vapor, arose from that little, teeny baby. The angels of God caught it, put it in the basket, closed the lid, and raised their hands toward heaven.

The angels began to shout praises to the Lord. They acclaimed Him and extolled Him as King of Kings and Lord of Lords, Creator of all things in heaven and earth. They shouted, "To God be the glory!"

As they came past us, they said again, "Come and see."

We went back through the gate into heaven. Oh, my! This seemed to be the most beautiful part of heaven! I had not been in this side of heaven or through this entrance.

I remember going with the angels to a certain place in heaven. I was accompanied by the angel who had been escorting me. We went so high up I could see the throne again, and I could hear the shouts and the praises of God. This time we seemed to approach from the left side of the throne.

I remember coming around this way and thinking, "Oh God, how beautiful You are. How wonderful You are." The high praises of God and the glory and the shouts were everywhere.

You know, the Holy Scriptures talk about the angels so much. Here are some examples:

> [20] *Bless the LORD, you His angels, who excel in strength, who do His word, heeding the voice of His word.*
>
> (Psalm 103:20)

> [7] *The angel of the LORD encamps all around those who fear Him, and delivers them.*   (Psalm 34:7)

> [2] *And behold, there was a great earthquake; for an angel of the Lord descended from heaven, and came and rolled back the stone from the door, and sat on it.*
> [3] *His countenance was like lightning, and his clothing as white as snow.*
>
> (Matthew 28:2–3)

Jesus talked about being carried by the angels to heaven:

> [22] *So it was that the beggar died, and was carried by the angels to Abraham's*

bosom. The rich man also died and was buried. (Luke 16:22)

ANGELS OF GOD

There are many references to angels in the Word of the Lord. I was just thinking about how His Word proves things over and over. But when a revelation is given to someone, it just sheds more light on it.

My primary calling in God is dreams, visions, and revelations. My testimony is that I am just a handmaiden of the Lord, and I just love to tell this story about the children.

Oh, the glory that we saw and the voices of praise that we heard! Around the throne were lightning and thunder and a rainbow. There was an image of a Man inside the cloud of glory that covered the throne.

The angels set the basket they carried down on the throne and bowed. Their wing tips went up. Shouts of "Glory!" and "Hallelujah! and "Praise God!" sounded all over heaven.

Again it seemed like we were in a huge arena. Large angels were blowing trumpets as if they were announcing something.

Now, I did not see God, but I saw the similarity of God just as Moses did. (See Exodus 33:17–23.) Then I saw a hand open up the basket. I am sure that it was the image of God's hand.

Dear one, I'm telling you, if you could only see the glory and the power of God just like He revealed it to me! His power was so dazzling and beautiful and wonderful!

I saw the hand come out of the cloud and open up the basket. It took that little soul out of the basket and laid it on the altar. Then I saw hands begin to work on this little soul.

When the task was finished and completed, the most beautiful, perfect form of a human began to appear. It continued to develop until it became the most handsome young man I have ever seen.

IN GOD'S CARE

There are no defects or marks of sin in heaven. The Scripture about Adam's creation came to me. Then the Lord said, "There are no imperfections in this place. Everything that was lost by the first Adam was restored by the second Adam."

It is my firm belief that the only signs of sin in heaven will be the scars in Jesus' hands and feet and side. This will be a reminder forever and forever that our blessed Lord paid the price for our redemption.

Then I saw what I perceived to be the top of God's head—it looked like wool (Revelation 1:14). A marvelous transformation took place as God breathed into this little baby, and it became a fully perfect creation.

The angels began to shout and praise God. As I watched this mighty manifestation of God's power, all of the questions that I have ever had about what happens to infants and children vanished completely. Now I know without a doubt that they are in the hands of God, being made into perfection!

Then the angel and I began to go high, high up the side of a place in heaven. There were beautiful trees everywhere with all kinds of fruit on them. I saw flowers of every description.

I could see all kinds of birds—some we have never seen before. Oh, the beauty of heaven is indescribable!

We went very high up to another part. I could hear the shouts of glory. A large angel wearing a long, white robe stood beside a gate. He was positioned behind a desk. He picked up a golden book from the desk and handed it to another angel.

The angel who received the book opened it, and shafts of brilliant, sparkling light issued from it and began to flash. It reminded me of millions of fireworks that were set off simultaneously.

Then I saw parents and family members as they began to move around and gravitate to certain individuals. They began to shout, leap, and jump. I could not understand what was taking place.

The angel said to me, "These loved ones are recognizing their family members." Those who had been dismembered, paralyzed, crippled, or had died prematurely were now in a state of perfection. They had been made whole!

In heaven, you will know everyone. You will know Abraham, Isaac, and Jacob. You will know Moses and all the prophets. You will know all the disciples of the New Testament.

You will know every person in heaven. You will know just as God knows you (1 Corinthians 13:12). You will have very extensive knowledge.

The angels said to me, "Come. You're going inside this gate."

It was the most beautiful gate I had seen in heaven. It was designed like a garden gate with wood around it, but it was made with what looked like whitish stone or marble. Beautiful flowers grew all around it.

We went through the gate and witnessed all the wonderful rejoicing and the reunion of all of God's family.

A HEAVENLY REUNION

King David knew very well that when little ones die prematurely for whatever reason, their souls go to heaven, where believing members of their families will be reunited with them some day. When his own infant son, who had been

conceived out of wedlock in an adulterous affair
with Bathsheba, died, David sincerely repented
of his sin and was certain that God had forgiven
him (Psalm 32:5). Because David found peace in
the knowledge that he would spend eternity
with God (see Psalm 23:6) and that he would see
his infant son again (2 Samuel 12:23), he was
able to comfort Bathsheba in her grief.

Here is the biblical account of the incident:

> [13] *So David said to Nathan, "I have
> sinned against the LORD." And Nathan
> said to David, "The LORD also has put
> away your sin; you shall not die.*
> [14] *"However, because by this deed you
> have given great occasion to the enemies
> of the LORD to blaspheme, the child also
> who is born to you shall surely die."*
> [16] *David therefore pleaded with God for
> the child, and David fasted and went in
> and lay all night on the ground.*
> [17] *So the elders of his house arose and
> went to him, to raise him up from the
> ground. But he would not, nor did he
> eat food with them.*
> [18] *Then on the seventh day it came to
> pass that the child died....*
> [19] *When David saw that his servants*

were whispering, David perceived that the child was dead. Therefore David said to his servants, "Is the child dead?" And they said, "He is dead."

²⁰ *So David arose from the ground, washed and anointed himself, and changed his clothes; and he went into the house of the LORD and worshiped. Then he went to his own house; and when he requested, they set food before him, and he ate.*

²¹ *Then his servants said to him, "What is this that you have done? You fasted and wept for the child while he was alive, but when the child died, you arose and ate food."*

²² *And he said, "While the child was alive, I fasted and wept; for I said, 'Who can tell whether the LORD will be gracious to me, that the child may live?'*

²³ *"But now he is dead; why should I fast? Can I bring him back again? I shall go to him, but he shall not return to me."*

²⁴ *Then David comforted Bathsheba his wife.* (2 Samuel 12:13–14, 16–24)

An angel of the Lord said to me, "From the time of conception, a baby is an eternal soul. If a baby is aborted or miscarried or somehow dies,

God knows about it. He has given His angels charge over them.

"We bring their little souls to heaven, and God completes them. It doesn't matter if a baby has been aborted or dies naturally. It is fashioned and formed into perfection by the mighty hand of God.

"If the parents of these children will live righteously in Christ Jesus, when they come to heaven, they will be reunited and will know their precious loved ones. They will meet them at the gates of glory!"

Seven

Worshipping around the Throne

Now, I praise God for the opportunity to put my vision of heaven in a book. It burns in my heart continually. Many people have encouraged me to write down this testimony and share the vision of heaven that God has given to me.

I have shared the heavenly vision, as well as my experiences of hell, in many churches where I have ministered.

I want to share with you some other scenes I saw in heaven. I want you to know that heaven is real. If you have lost a loved one, someone who has gone on before you to heaven, that person will meet you at the gates of glory. I want to encourage your heart, because we have a blessed hope in Jesus Christ. He has gone to heaven to prepare a place for us there.

The angels I saw in heaven seemed to be very large and mighty! They wore glistening, shimmering robes that radiated huge amounts of light. They were powerful and sincere. They had their minds set to obey God. It was obvious to me that the mighty angels I saw at each gate of pearl were protecting angels.

As I saw the swords by the angels' sides, I thought, "Well, glory to God! Hallelujah! God surely does protect His children."

THE ANGELS OF GOD

You know, the Bible talks about angels so much, with many passages referring to angels. It is amazing that sometimes we tend to overlook

things that God's Word proves over and over.
When a revelation is given to someone, however,
this seems to shed more light on the subject.

Here are some more examples of what the
Bible says about angels:

> 11 *For He shall give His angels charge
> over you, to keep you in all your ways.*
> 12 *In their hands they shall bear you up,
> lest you dash your foot against a stone.*
> (Psalm 91:11–12)

> 40 *The LORD, before whom I walk, will
> send His angel with you and prosper
> your way.* (Genesis 24:40)

> 1 *I saw still another mighty angel coming
> down from heaven, clothed with a cloud.
> And a rainbow was on his head, his face
> was like the sun, and his feet like pillars
> of fire.* (Revelation 10:1)

> 1 *After these things I saw another angel
> coming down from heaven, having great
> authority, and the earth was illumi-
> nated with his glory.* (Revelation 18:1)

> 25 *For when they rise from the dead,
> they neither marry nor are given in
> marriage, but are like angels in heaven.*
> (Mark 12:25)

43 Then an angel appeared to Him from heaven, strengthening Him.

(Luke 22:43)

14 Are [angels] not all ministering spirits sent forth to minister for those who will inherit salvation? (Hebrews 1:14)

10 Likewise, I say to you, there is joy in the presence of the angels of God over one sinner who repents. (Luke 15:10)

Again I was allowed to enter through the gate of heaven, and I remember I was overwhelmed with feeling the peace and joy that are there. Oh, the glorious singing and the praises! Saints, I don't think anybody could describe it very well, because earth has never felt a peace such as this. Since Eden, earth has never experienced the peace, the joy, and the rest that are in heaven.

In heaven there is no sickness. In heaven there are no wheelchairs. In heaven there are no disabilities. In heaven there are no diseases. All is perfect and beautiful. There is no corruption. There are no lies. There is no sin, because God will not allow one sin to enter the gates of heaven.

THE GRAND SPECTACULAR

With the angel guiding me, we moved very quickly. We passed many fruit trees that grew beside the River of Life. Every one of them was loaded with beautiful fruit.

As we moved along, it seemed that we became part of the music. At all times in heaven, I heard music, and it was always new. I heard continuous musical praises being lifted in honor and praise to God.

The angel of God said to me, "We are going before the throne to see the worship of God." Along the way, it seemed like hundreds of people were coming from all over heaven. They were going to worship the King of Kings and the Lord of Lords.

WORSHIP IN HEAVEN

As we moved along, it seemed as if the hundreds turned into thousands, and the thousands into an innumerable host. They appeared from different parts of heaven. Apparently we went to the large arena-type area that John described:

² *Immediately I was in the Spirit; and behold, a throne set in heaven, and One sat on the throne.*
³ *And He who sat there was like a jasper and a sardius stone in appearance; and there was a rainbow around the throne, in appearance like an emerald.*
⁴ *Around the throne were twenty-four thrones, and on the thrones I saw twenty-four elders sitting, clothed in white robes; and they had crowns of gold on their heads.*
⁵ *And from the throne proceeded lightnings, thunderings, and voices. Seven lamps of fire were burning before the throne, which are the seven Spirits of God.*
¹⁰ *The twenty-four elders fall down before Him who sits on the throne and worship Him who lives forever and ever, and cast their crowns before the throne, saying:*
¹¹ *"You are worthy, O Lord, to receive glory and honor and power; for You created all things, and by Your will they exist and were created."*

(Revelation 4:2–5, 10–11)

And the clouds! The most beautiful clouds were billowing in and out around the throne.

Shaped almost like the mushroom cloud of an atomic explosion, each cloud was mixed with glory and beautiful colors.

A dazzling rainbow arched above all of this. It is impossible to imagine the intensity of the power of God.

I knew in my heart that the image of the man that I saw in the clouds was the representation of God.

Thousands of years ago, God wanted to make a man in His image, and He did it.

> [27] *So God created man in His own image; in the image of God He created him; male and female He created them.*
> (Genesis 1:27)

God literally took the dirt from the ground and made a man. Think about the power of God that must have been present:

> [7] *And the LORD God formed man of the dust of the ground, and breathed into his nostrils the breath of life; and man became a living being.*   (Genesis 2:7)

Then, because Adam was alone—*"But for Adam there was not found a helper comparable to him"* (Genesis 2:20)—God put him into a deep sleep. God opened up Adam's side, removed one of Adam's ribs, and fashioned a woman from it. God formed Eve, Adam's lifelong companion and mate, who was also made in God's image (Genesis 1:27). What glory was given to human beings to be made in God's image!

PREPARING FOR THE KING

The testimonies of heavenly worship show the beauty and the holiness of God. As we arrived at the place of assembly, I could see people and angels everywhere. I was impressed that everything was done in order. Everywhere, people and angels praised God.

The River of Life flowed forth from the throne of God. It was like a sea of glass, like a sea of crystal, but it was flowing.

Then, saints, again I saw horses. The big, white, magnificent horses looked as though they were made out of marble. They were beautiful and without a single flaw in any of them. They were elegant, like chess pieces, but they were physically real.

The white blankets on the horses' backs were neatly trimmed with gold edging. Golden reins were in their mouths. They had ornaments on their feet and even on the brush of their tails. These horses stood alert before the throne.

I noticed that the twelve angels standing before the throne had trumpets and musical horns by their sides. Their flowing, glowing garments were trimmed with gold and embedded with big rubies and all kinds of immense stones.

Suddenly, I saw many musical instruments. They were the most spectacular instruments you could ever imagine seeing. Oh, the beauty of heaven! There were many harps. I looked to see who was stationed at these musical instruments.

I thought, "Oh, glory to God! Hallelujah!"

CALL TO WORSHIP

Then, saints, the Holy Spirit very clearly showed me something. The woman who was in the center of the group of horses stood still. Then the angels in front of the throne, each one in order, picked up the trumpet or horn by his side and began to blow. When they blew these horns—oh, the sounds of joy and high praise that went up! Someone in heaven loudly proclaimed:

> It is now time to worship the King of Kings and the Lord of Lords for His glorious acts and His glorious power unto the people of the earth.
>
> It is time to give Him high praise, to worship Him in the song and the dance, to worship Him with music, and to worship Him for His goodness.
>
> He is God. He is King of Kings and Lord of Lords. He is the Redeemer of mankind.

As they announced these things, saints, the trumpets were sounding! Then the angel who was reading the scroll stopped, and a signal was given.

Immediately, those magnificent horses all bowed their knees. Their heads went down all in a row in praise to the name of the Lord:

> [10] *At the name of Jesus every knee should bow, of those in heaven, and of*

*those on earth, and of those under the
earth.* (Philippians 2:10)

[13] *Every creature which is in heaven and
on the earth and under the earth and
such as are in the sea, and all that are in
them, I heard saying: "Blessing and
honor and glory and power be to Him
who sits on the throne, and to the Lamb,
forever and ever!"* (Revelation 5:13)

The horses then began to spin and prance
before the Lord. They did all kinds of things to
magnify and praise and worship God. Oh, if only
you could have seen it! And God was pleased
with their worship unto Him.

MOTIVATION TO PRAISE

Saints, I don't think we realize how much
God loves our praises. When we are going
through trials, heartaches, and sorrows, God
wants us to praise Him. We are to praise Him,
not because of the sorrows or the trials, but because we love Him.

When we worship Him, we seem to do so
for His sake, not for our own. As we praise Him
for the mighty things He has done for us, we

shift our focus from ourselves to God. In the process of entering into worship, we come to realize that He is the One who can solve the problems we are facing, and we can trust Him to come to our aid. So, we actually benefit when we truly praise and worship the Lord.

ACCOLADES OF PRAISE

At that time, all the heavenly musicians began to play, and another group of worshippers came in. Thousands of voices sang in honor and praise to Jesus. The sounds of glorious shouting went up. There was ringing all over heaven. For hours, it seemed, praises rang out to God!

How beautiful it is to hear and to be in the midst of praises to God! There, in the center of the resonating, magnificent sounds, the earth seemed so far away to me. Sorrows and troubles seemed so far away. The horrors of hell seemed so far away.

MY ASSIGNMENT FROM GOD

However, I knew within myself that I had something to do for God. The angel of God touched me, and strength came into me.

He said to me, "Child, God has allowed you to see these things so that you can tell them and can record them. Revelations and visions and dreams are given to you to let the people on earth know *'the things which God has prepared for those...who love Him and keep His commandments'*" (1 Corinthians 2:9; Deuteronomy 7:9).

Then, saints, I heard God's voice! Just the sound of His voice filled me with ecstasy. It sounded like thunder, but I could understand what He was saying.

I fell on my face and began to worship and praise the King of Kings and Lord of Lords.

HEAVENLY SCRIPTURES

When I returned to the earth and began to ponder the many wonderful things God had shown me, I looked in the Word of God. It seemed that everywhere I turned, I was reading something about heaven and God's majesty.

I want to share a few of those Scripture verses with you:

⁶ *You alone are the LORD; You have made heaven, the heaven of heavens, with all their host, the earth and everything on it, the seas and all that is in them, and You preserve them all. The host of heaven worships You.*

(Nehemiah 9:6)

¹² *Is not God in the height of heaven?...*
¹⁴ *"Thick clouds cover Him, so that He cannot see, and He walks above the circle of heaven."* (Job 22:12, 14)

¹⁹ *For He looked down from the height of His sanctuary; from heaven the LORD viewed the earth.* (Psalm 102:19)

¹⁹ *The LORD has established His throne in heaven, and His kingdom rules over all.* (Psalm 103:19)

¹³ *Let them praise the name of the LORD, for His name alone is exalted; His glory is above the earth and heaven.*

(Psalm 148:13)

²² *But you have come to Mount Zion and to the city of the living God, the heavenly Jerusalem, to an innumerable company of angels.* (Hebrews 12:22)

Eight

Holy Creatures in Heaven

This is a true account of an experience that happened to me. Once again, the angel of the Lord came to me and said, "Behold the glory of your God."

I was taken up instantly into the heavenlies and through one of the gates into heaven. Each gate was made of an exquisite pearl, with designs in it. The beauty of heaven is stunning!

We passed the River of Life, and I could hear people shouting on the banks of the river and praising God. I was taken before the throne of God as it is described in the fourth chapter of Revelation. Oh, what shouts and what worship!

Saints, I saw the throne of God just like Holy Scripture says. It has a rainbow around it. It is overshadowed with the cloud of glory and the brilliance of the power of God. I heard voices, saw lightning, and heard thunder. I saw the divine manifestations of the power of God!

> *5 And from the throne proceeded lightnings, thunderings, and voices. Seven lamps of fire were burning before the throne, which are the seven Spirits of God.*
> *6 Before the throne there was a sea of glass, like crystal. And in the midst of the throne, and around the throne, were four living creatures full of eyes in front and in back.* (Revelation 4:5–6)

As I looked, I heard the multiplied voices of many angels around the throne. The number of angels there was inestimable. Then I saw the heavenly creatures and the elders. There were four of the heavenly creatures and twenty-four elders. This scene was also described by John in Revelation:

> [11] *Then I looked, and I heard the voice of many angels around the throne, the living creatures, and the elders; and the number of them was ten thousand times ten thousand, and thousands of thousands.* (Revelation 5:11)

> [11] *All the angels stood around the throne and the elders and the four living creatures, and fell on their faces before the throne and worshiped God.* (Revelation 7:11)

THE LIVING CREATURES

On this particular trip to the throne of God, I saw the four living creatures that were before the throne of God. These creatures I saw around the throne were the ones written about in the Word of God.

All of the heavenly creatures had large eyes, some in the front and some in the back. They could see in the front of them and behind them. They were very large and unlike anything

I have ever seen on earth.

Each of them had six wings. One had the face of a lion. The second had a face like a calf.

The third living creature had a face like a man. Imagine, if you can, a very tall creature with six wings. It has the face of a man. The fourth living creature was like a flying eagle.

All of these fascinating creatures were constantly crying out, *"Holy, holy, holy, Lord God Almighty."*

Since I had never before seen any creature that resembled them in appearance, they looked very strange to me. I knew, however, that God had created these holy creatures in heaven. I praise God for His mighty acts and His mighty power. God is an awesome God! As I watched these creatures, they began to praise and worship God Almighty.

I want you to understand that after I saw the heavenly creatures of God in my vision, I made a study about them and discovered John's amazing description of what I had witnessed in the book of Revelation. Here is how John described them:

⁶ Before the throne there was a sea of glass, like crystal. And in the midst of the throne, and around the throne, were four living creatures full of eyes in front and in back.

⁷ The first living creature was like a lion, the second living creature like a calf, the third living creature had a face like a man, and the fourth living creature was like a flying eagle.

⁸ The four living creatures, each having six wings, were full of eyes around and within. And they do not rest day or night, saying: "Holy, holy, holy, Lord God Almighty, Who was and is and is to come!" (Revelation 4:6–8)

THE DUTIES OF THE LIVING CREATURES

The Bible tells us about these living creatures and their duties. They continuously give God praise and honor. Along with the twenty-four elders, worshipping the Lord is their main occupation:

⁸ The four living creatures...do not rest day or night, saying: "Holy, holy, holy, Lord God Almighty, Who was and is and is to come!"

⁹ *Whenever the living creatures give glory and honor and thanks to Him who sits on the throne, who lives forever and ever,*
¹⁰ *the twenty-four elders fall down before Him who sits on the throne and worship Him who lives forever and ever, and cast their crowns before the throne, saying:*
¹¹ *"You are worthy, O Lord, to receive glory and honor and power; for You created all things, and by Your will they exist and were created."*

(Revelation 4:8–11)

⁹ *And they* [the four living creatures and the twenty-four elders] *sang a new song: "You are worthy to take the scroll and to open its seals, because you were slain, and with your blood you purchased men for God from every tribe and language and people and nation.*
¹⁰ *"You have made them to be a kingdom and priests to serve our God, and they will reign on the earth."*

(Revelation 5:9–10 NIV)

¹¹ *Then I looked, and I heard the voice of many angels around the throne, the living creatures, and the elders; and the number of them was ten thousand times*

*ten thousand, and thousands of thou-
sands,*
[12] *saying with a loud voice: "Worthy is
the Lamb who was slain to receive power
and riches and wisdom, and strength
and honor and glory and blessing!"*
[13] *And every creature which is in heaven
and on the earth and under the earth
and such as are in the sea, and all that
are in them, I heard saying: "Blessing
and honor and glory and power be to
Him who sits on the throne, and to the
Lamb, forever and ever!"*
[14] *Then the four living creatures said,
"Amen!" And the twenty-four elders fell
down and worshiped Him who lives
forever and ever.* (Revelation 5:11–14)

[11] *All the angels stood around the
throne and the elders and the four living creatures, and fell on their faces before the throne and worshiped God,*
[12] *saying: "Amen! Blessing and glory
and wisdom, thanksgiving and honor
and power and might, be to our God
forever and ever. Amen."*

(Revelation 7:11–12)

[4] *And the twenty-four elders and the
four living creatures fell down and
worshiped God who sat on the throne,*

saying, "Amen! Alleluia!"
⁵ Then a voice came from the throne, saying, "Praise our God, all you His servants and those who fear Him, both small and great!"
⁶ And I heard, as it were, the voice of a great multitude, as the sound of many waters and as the sound of mighty thunderings, saying, "Alleluia! For the Lord God Omnipotent reigns!"
(Revelation 19:4–6)

Other duties of the living creatures are also described in Revelation:

⁸ Now when He had taken the scroll, the four living creatures and the twenty-four elders fell down before the Lamb, each having a harp, and golden bowls full of incense, which are the prayers of the saints.   (Revelation 5:8)

¹ Now I saw when the Lamb opened one of the seals; and I heard one of the four living creatures saying with a voice like thunder, "Come and see."
(Revelation 6:1)

⁶ And out of the temple came the seven angels having the seven plagues, clothed in pure bright linen, and having

their chests girded with golden bands.
⁷ Then one of the four living creatures
gave to the seven angels seven golden
bowls full of the wrath of God who lives
forever and ever.
⁸ The temple was filled with smoke from
the glory of God and from His power,
and no one was able to enter the temple
till the seven plagues of the seven angels
were completed.   (Revelation 15:6–8)

I saw an innumerable multitude of angels as they began to worship the Lord. I heard and experienced the unforgettable scene as the elders around the throne joined in. I, too, joined in worshipping the King, as I thought, "Oh, how glorious to see the power of Almighty God!"

Nine

The Glories of Heaven

W hen Jesus Christ revealed heaven to me, I was taken there for ten visits by the power of God Almighty. It happened immediately after the time He showed me hell.

The divine visits began during the Easter season. Jesus appeared to me from 2 A.M. to 5 A.M. every night for thirty nights, showing me the destination of those who reject Him. Before I saw heaven, He took me into the center of the earth and showed me the abode of the dead.

I wrote *A Divine Revelation of Hell,* in which I related my experiences in hell. After those thirty trips into the depths of horror, for ten nights Jesus showed me heaven and its glories. Additionally, there were many other visitations from the Lord.

This is a true account of what happened to me. The Spirit of the living God revealed to me everything I am telling you.

When Jesus Christ took me on these journeys, I was fascinated because in heaven, there is no sorrow, no death, no dying, and no grief. In heaven only joy, peace, happiness, and the fruits of the Spirit are everywhere.

I was also fascinated by the angels of God who were there by the thousands. Some had wings; some didn't.

I noticed on every one of my journeys to heaven that the angels were always busy. The angels performed tasks and took care of details constantly. It seemed to me that each angel had his particular assignments and certain jobs to do. But all of them were always praising God and performing their duties happily as they went about their business.

All of the angels are constantly occupied with their duties. For example, when new souls come to heaven, angels meet them and lead them immediately through the River of Life. The angels escort the new souls to a place where other angels outfit them with gowns of salvation, which are robes of righteousness. Then the angelic guides take them to the room of crowns, where each person is fitted with a crown.

All of these things are done in beautiful, perfect order. The angels are perfectly happy while doing them.

I never saw bells in heaven, but I heard them ringing constantly. I was told that every time a bell rings, a soul on earth was just saved. This is called "the glories of heaven."

HEAVENLY FURNISHINGS

I noticed that all during my trips to heaven, I saw beautiful tables. I don't know how to describe them adequately.

Sometimes on earth I have seen Victorian or some other style of furniture with elaborate designs on the pieces. You have probably seen such beautiful pieces, like a table against the side of a wall as you walk by or a table with a vase or book on it. Well, in heaven I saw tables like these everywhere, except they were even more exquisitely designed and made.

There were also books everywhere, as well as many other things.

HEAVENLY RECORDINGS

Saints, be aware that every time you give money, every time you pay tithes, everything you do for the glory of God is recorded in heaven. I remember this so well because when the Lord showed me His mighty glories and powers, it made an impression that will never be erased from my mind.

During my trips, I noticed that many angels came to heaven with reports from all over the earth. They would go to a certain room with a recording angel in charge. The messenger angel would read the report, and the recording angel would ask, "Are you a witness? Did you see this take place?"

When the report was confirmed, it was logged in a book. These books were eventually taken to the throne of God. But first, they had to go through a special process.

I vividly remember that the Spirit of the Lord moved continuously in heaven. It was greater than anything on earth. Things on earth are patterned after things in heaven, but the earthly things can only be shadowy reflections of those in heaven. Unbelievable music, unhindered praises, and other glories that the earth can never imagine abound in heaven.

God wants people to praise Him. From the opening of Genesis to the close of Revelation, God expressed His desire for a family to love Him.

As you read this book, remember that heaven is a place God has prepared for those who love Him. Someday I am going there. Someday you are going there if you are born again, if you have repented of your sins, and if you have Jesus Christ in your heart.

He can wash your sins away through His precious blood. Let me tell you of the blood of the Lamb, the precious blood of Jesus.

THE CLEANSING BLOOD

Earlier, I described the record rooms, but now I want to depict another aspect. A number of angels sat in a certain section of the record rooms. They had golden buckets in front of them. This is also a part of "the glories of heaven."

In front of the angels were stacks of books. Some of the markers in the books seemed to be messages from earth. Each message had to be examined by a large recording angel.

I saw two other angels who brought messages from earth. There was a new message every time someone was born again, having been truly saved from his sins by accepting Jesus Christ into his heart. When someone truly repented of his sins and asked Jesus to be his Savior and Lord, it was recorded that the person had given his life to the Lord.

The angels with the golden buckets each took a book from the stack. Each angel held in his hands what looked like a bloodstained cloth. The red cloth was mixed with glory, light, and power. It was not gory or anything like that—it was beautiful!

Each angel positioned the selected book in front of him, and, starting at the first page, he expunged the written record with the blood-stained cloth. With God's direction, the angel erased the old history of this sinner and recorded that he or she had just been born again.

> ²⁵ *I, even I, am He who blots out your transgressions for My own sake; and I will not remember your sins.*
>
> (Isaiah 43:25)

Children, the Word of God is true. God truly forgives our sins. It was so beautiful to see the angels washing the pages. Hallelujah, God wipes the slate clean for each of us!

As I saw this glorious thing, I heard the saints in glory sing:

> Oh, nothing but the blood of Jesus
> Can wash my sins away.
> Oh, nothing but the blood of Jesus
> Can make me whole today.
> Oh, nothing but the blood of Jesus
> Can cleanse me today.

And then I heard the angels singing this song:

Another one's been redeemed
By the blood of the Lamb.
Another one's been saved from the
Devil's hand
By the blood of the Lamb.
Another one's been saved from hell
By the blood of Jesus Christ.

Never be ashamed to call upon the power of the blood of Jesus Christ. His blood was shed almost two thousand years ago to wash away our sins, and it has never lost its power since then! Jesus conquered the Devil *"once for all when He offered up Himself"* (Hebrews 7:27) and went to the cross for us.

Christ came down from glory. He was born of a virgin. He gave His life in order that we could be redeemed by His precious blood. He did this so that we would not have to go to hell, the awful place He showed to me.

Dear friends, the Gospel is true. How I rejoiced when I saw the angels washing away all of the old history from the stacks of books. They erased all the old past, all the old sins, all the dirty things. All the old things were gone; the blood of Jesus eradicated them all.

Only Jesus can do this for you. You cannot do it yourself.

ALTARS OF GOD

I love the altars of God. When I go to a Spirit-filled church that has a beautiful altar, I know that many tears have been shed there.

In the Old Testament, God repeatedly commanded His people to go in and tear down the old heathen altars. Here is one example:

> [3] *And you shall destroy their altars, break their sacred pillars, and burn their wooden images with fire; you shall cut down the carved images of their gods and destroy their names from that place.*
> [4] *You shall not worship the LORD your God with such things.*
> (Deuteronomy 12:3–4)

God's people were to get rid of the sinful altars that did not give praise to Him. They were to remove the altars that did not honor or reverence Him, and then they were to build and keep altars only for His worship. Here is an example of those instructions:

25 *Now it came to pass the same night that the LORD said to [Joshua], "Take your father's young bull, the second bull of seven years old, and tear down the altar of Baal that your father has, and cut down the wooden image that is beside it;* 26 *"and build an altar to the LORD your God on top of this rock in the proper arrangement, and take the second bull and offer a burnt sacrifice with the wood of the image which you shall cut down."* (Judges 6:25–26)

TODAY'S ALTARS

When I preach in services across the country, I think of the altars of God. When we come to the front altar of a church and pour out our hearts to God, we are not ashamed of Him. A dedicated altar is one place where we can be in the presence of God, where we can call on Him and confess our sins, asking Him to forgive us.

Many of us feel His awesome presence there! We can know He answers our prayers. At times we can feel His arms around us. There is something wonderful about the altars—the old-fashioned altars of God—in churches. There you can go and kneel and just worship the Lord.

You can praise God at home, too. You can do it in your car. You can praise Him anywhere. However, let me tell you something: the altar is a definite place for an appointment to commune with Him intimately.

When the Old Testament prophets made altars to God, they cried out and repented to God for the sins of the people as well as for their own sins. At the altar they repented and offered blood sacrifices on behalf of the people, and God accepted their sacrifices.

Since Christ made the ultimate sacrifice for our sins through His shed blood, we no longer need to offer sacrifices. However, we still need to repent when we are convicted of sin, and one of the best places to do that is at an altar. When we see a dedicated church altar, we should kneel at it and pray to God, if it is possible.

It means so much to have an altar. We need one in our homes, so we can talk to God and have a place just to be with Him.

When I preach I always tell the people, "Don't be ashamed to come to this altar. Here God will meet you."

Yes, He can meet you in your seat. Nevertheless, there is something about a sanctified and often-used altar where you can humble yourself, raise your hands, and say, "God, here I am. Take me. Use me for Your glory."

WORSHIP HIM SINCERELY

You need to mean what you pray with all your heart. God is looking for a people to love Him and to praise Him. God is looking for a people who will turn from their wicked ways and come back to Him. He is looking for a people who will worship Him in spirit and in truth.

[14] *If My people who are called by My name will humble themselves, and pray and seek My face, and turn from their wicked ways, then I will hear from heaven, and will forgive their sin and heal their land.* (2 Chronicles 7:14)

[23] *But the hour is coming, and now is, when the true worshipers will worship the Father in spirit and truth; for the Father is seeking such to worship Him.* [24] *God is Spirit, and those who worship Him must worship in spirit and truth.*
(John 4:23–24)

Be honest with God. Be truthful with God. When you go to the altar, don't kneel and say, "Betty did wrong," or "Joe did wrong." Say, "God, I am the one who sinned. I'm standing in the need of forgiveness." Then, forgive those whom you have something against—forgive them.

Saints, the Lord is looking for a people of deliverance, so that the blind eyes will be opened and ears will hear what the Spirit of the Lord is saying to the churches (Revelation 2:7).

Oh, the glories of heaven! If you could only see what awaits you there!

We go through many trials and tribulations in everyday life. Sometimes it seems that the Enemy tries to steal everything from us, but God gives us the patience to endure and, ultimately, the victory. There are many pressures of life, but in our Lord there is peace and safety.

If you don't have a good, solid, home church, I urge you to search for one that preaches the true Word of God and believes in the power of the Almighty to transform lives and hearts. Find a church that believes in the power of the Holy Spirit. There you will be taught the wisdom of God and can be set free from your troubles, sorrows, and grief.

You know, it is important to meet together with God's people. The Bible tells us to assemble ourselves together (Hebrews 10:25). Don't try to be out there all alone. God loves you, and there are saints of God who love you, too.

GLORIES TO BE REVEALED

Another part of the glories of heaven included some of the mysteries that are yet to be revealed. I was not allowed to see them.

However, on one of the trips, I saw beautiful houses and mansions. This part seemed to go by very fast. Then I was taken to where I saw angels doing all kinds of tasks. They seemed to be coming from the earth in an orderly manner, and they would come into the gates with papers in their hands.

Sometimes the angels would have books in which they had been writing. They would go to certain areas in heaven with these reports. Then the reports would be logged in books, to keep records for the saints' rewards.

When you go to heaven, you will be rewarded for whatever you do for Jesus Christ's sake. This is why I write this book. I am writing of my visions of heaven for the sake of the Lord Jesus Christ and for His glory and honor.

I want you to understand the part of the mysteries of heaven that God showed me. I can only tell you what I saw, for the mysteries were revealed to me only in part. The Bible says that now *"we know in part, and we prophesy in part"* (1 Corinthians 13:9).

Praise God, when we reach our final destination, our final home, all of our questions will be answered, all of our prayers will be answered, and all of our deepest desires will be fulfilled!

Ten

Visions of Angels at Work

I n this chapter I want to tell you about my
visions of angels at work. I want you to understand some of the beautiful things God has
shown me. I want to give you some joy and de-
light in knowing what awaits you as you are
working for the Lord.

God is wonderful to reveal *"His secret to
His servants the prophets"* (Amos 3:7). His desire is to show these things to those who will be

sensitive to His revelations and who will proclaim His message.

> [6] *Thus says the LORD, the King of Israel, and his Redeemer, the LORD of hosts: "I am the First and I am the Last; besides Me there is no God.*
> [7] *"And who can proclaim as I do? Then let him declare it and set it in order for Me, since I appointed the ancient people. And the things that are coming and shall come, let them show these to them.*
> [8] *"Do not fear, nor be afraid; have I not told you from that time, and declared it? You are My witnesses. Is there a God besides Me? Indeed there is no other Rock; I know not one."* (Isaiah 44:6–8)

> [2] *Then the LORD answered me and said: "Write the vision and make it plain on tablets, that he may run who reads it."*
> (Habakkuk 2:2)

There are many scriptural examples about God wanting to reveal things to us through His appointed representatives. The Word of God is sure and true.

According to the Bible, Daniel had visions from the Lord:

¹ *Daniel had a dream, and visions passed through his mind as he was lying on his bed. He wrote down the substance of his dream.* (Daniel 7:1 NIV)

John the Revelator also saw visions of the Lord, and he was told to write them down: *"What you see, write in a book"* (Revelation 1:11).

Isaiah was a great prophet with a crucial message for Judah because of his visions and his courage in telling them. His book begins: *"The vision of Isaiah the son of Amoz, which he saw concerning Judah and Jerusalem"* (Isaiah 1:1).

Because Ezekiel saw visions of God (Ezekiel 1:1), he was called and anointed for a prophetic ministry.

God, in His infinite mercy, has seen fit to choose me and show me visions from Himself. I praise God for this. When I am in prayer and meditation, seeking God on certain matters, I am allowed to see into mysteries by the Spirit. He reveals certain things to me.

My calling in God is to receive dreams, visions, and revelations and to relate them to others. As the Lord's anointed handmaiden, I am simply describing the things that He has shown to me. I believe this is my biblical role.

REVEALING GOD'S TRUTHS

At the start of these experiences, the Lord Jesus Christ appeared to me to show me hell. He appeared in a glistening white robe, full of light and power. Jesus seemed to me to be about six feet tall. His beard appeared as if it had been neatly trimmed. His thick hair rested lightly on His shoulders. His beautiful eyes were piercing.

The portrait of Christ that is closest to the way I saw Him in my visions shows Him on the Wailing Wall, praying over the Jews and Israel. Jesus Christ has so much love and compassion for us, as the artist portrayed in that portrait, that He will go to great lengths to show a person hell and heaven and things to come.

CHARIOTS OF FIRE

Look at what the Bible says:

17 And Elisha prayed, and said, "LORD, I pray, open his eyes that he may see." Then the LORD opened the eyes of the

young man, and he saw. And behold,
the mountain was full of horses and
chariots of fire all around Elisha.

(2 Kings 6:17)

When I was in heaven, I saw chariots of
fire, with angels driving the chariots. They were
very large vehicles, and I marveled at their
splendor.

REVELATIONS OF GOD

Look at this Bible verse about angels:

[10] *And while they looked steadfastly to-*
ward heaven as He went up, behold, two
men stood by them in white apparel.

(Acts 1:10)

How can one read that and not believe it?
God openly showed angels to His people when
Jesus was caught up to heaven.

Saints, we have to realize that God wants
to reveal His glorious powers and His wondrous
works in these last days. God has visions to
show us. He wants to communicate these truths
to us so that we can be excited and delighted
about working for Him on this earth.

MIRACLES IN CHURCH

After the time of these visions, I was ministering in a particular church service. I had been in deep prayer and meditation. At church that night, I saw angels everywhere. They all had golden swords in their hands.

The Spirit of the Lord spoke to me. He said to me in a clear way:

> Child, when prayer time comes for the people, I want to heal certain physical problems. I want this to be a sign in your ministry that the testimony of hell is true. I have given My word that I will give signs and wonders and work miracles as the Gospel of the Lord Jesus Christ is preached.

I became so excited! In my spirit I saw an angel with a large book writing down things as I preached. It seemed as if the ceiling opened up, and I could see a vision of the throne of God. Angels were rejoicing and praising God.

BREAKING THE BONDAGE OF SIN

When it was time for the altar call, I saw angels going among the congregation, nudging people to go to the altar and give their hearts to the Lord. When I saw the angels touching the hearts of individuals, the blackest sins began to churn up and out of their hearts as they knelt and prayed to God. Oh, it was beautiful!

In my spirit I could see chains that were wrapped around the people. As people received forgiveness, angels seemed to break the bondage, to shatter the chains, to cast them off. The bands broke as people began to raise their hands and confess their sins to the Lord.

Cries and shouts went up everywhere from souls who had been delivered. It was wonderful. In many of my services all over the world, God provided great miracles like these, and wonderful deliverances began to happen.

I praise God for His signs, wonders, and miracles. I know that the angels are at work, helping me with the ministry of the Lord Jesus Christ.

BREAKING THE BONDAGE

I want to tell you something else. As Scripture was being spoken, the Word seemed to jump off the page and take the form of a sword. That sword would pierce a person's body and go straight to the problem to heal it.

The glory of God was everywhere! I was amazed. I praise God for the blessings of heaven on earth and for this beautiful revelation of His Word.

Eleven

The Word of God

In many services where I go, I see so many beautiful things that the angels are doing. You know, of course, that the angels are ministering spirits of the Lord sent forth to minister to the heirs of salvation. (See Hebrews 1:13–14.)

Once I saw a minister prophesying. As he was prophesying, God opened up my eyes to see an angel over his head. The angel was pouring on him what looked like oil mingled with fire, out of a horn.

Then I saw the man's heart in a vision. It was full of the Bible, the Word of God. The Word seemed to come up from his heart, into his throat, and out his mouth. I could see the Word as it came out of his mouth. As it hit the air, it seemed to become a two-edged sword.

Another angel was recording what the man of God said.

I thought, "Oh, God, this is truly your Word going forth to the people."

Then I saw one of the angels holding the Holy Scriptures. As the man began to preach the living Word of God, the words seemed to leap off the pages of the Bible. They would go into his heart and out of his mouth. As this happened, the words of the Bible became a two-edged sword.

As the minister prayed for people who were sick or afflicted with diseases, it seemed that the Lord allowed me to see a dark spot in a lung, a leg, a heart, or wherever the affliction was. The sword of the Word would go to the affected place in the body, and heat would begin to form around it.

Many times when people are prayed over for healing, they say, "Oh, my, I feel the heat of the Spirit."

I was allowed to see spiritually how disease was really burned out of a person's body. It was so beautiful how the revelation of God's Word began to work. As I saw new skin and new cells began to grow where the old had been, I began to praise the Lord.

Later, as I talked to some of them, they would say to me, "I was miraculously healed that day."

Here on earth, we see only in part and know only in part. We see and know only what God allows. What I saw was only as God permitted, and I give Him all the credit, the honor, and the glory.

APPROACHING THE THRONE

I began to see the importance of and the need for prophets in today's world as well as in biblical times. I began to see the importance of all of the fivefold ministries spoken of in Ephesians:

169

> [11] *And He Himself gave some to be apostles, some prophets, some evangelists, and some pastors and teachers,*
> [12] *For the equipping of the saints for the work of ministry, for the edifying of the body of Christ.* (Ephesians 4:11–12)

I saw how important each is in the body of Christ.

The Bible tells us that we can *"come boldly to the throne of grace, that we may obtain mercy and find grace to help in time of need"* (Hebrews 4:16). The Word assures us that we have *"boldness to enter into the Holiest by the blood of Jesus"* (Hebrews 10:19), because *"according to the law almost all things are purified with blood, and without shedding of blood there is no remission"* (Hebrews 9:22).

Friends, I can attest that this is true. It is the blood of Jesus Christ that makes atonement for the soul. His Word and His blood work together in grace.

> [16] *Let us therefore come boldly to the throne of grace, that we may obtain mercy and find grace to help in time of need.* (Hebrews 4:16)

A VERY PRESENT HELP

How many times do we have great needs? We have sickness in our bodies. We are going through heartaches. We are going through a divorce. A loved one has died. A child has strayed into the world. It seems like we have no money coming in at all, and we need help. At times like these we come boldly to the throne of God and pray, "God, I need your help."

In the visions God gave me of scenes on earth, every time the saints would cry out to the Lord for help, the Word of God would be there. An angel would have a huge Bible in his hands. Then I would see the angel open the Word of God and shove it in Satan's face. Satan would be there in the form of an evil spirit or a serpent. When the angel opened up the Scriptures, the Devil would literally fall backward, screaming, because he knew the angel was using the two-edged sword against him.

Now, I need to tell you that the things that I was seeing in my spirit were not always happening in the church where I was ministering at the time. I would see things in my spirit that

171

could be occurring miles away. At times I did not know where or when they were taking place.

Thank God, Jesus has defeated Satan for us once and for all at the cross so that we can have freedom and life. We can now come boldly to the throne of grace wherever we are.

ANOINTING AND HEALING

God's mercy and grace is real and present to heal every sickness and disease through His Holy Scriptures. I want you to be encouraged in the Word of God today.

If you have a need, go boldly to the throne of grace and ask God to help you. The angels of God are *"ministering spirits sent forth to minister for those who will inherit salvation"* (Hebrews 1:14).

I am aware of this from Scripture, and I believe it. Moreover, I know it for a fact. I have seen it in the spirit realm many times. When we call on the Lord, God sends angels to help us in the power and might of His Word and His Spirit.

When demons have been cast out of someone in a service, I have seen the evil spirits come out like dark shadows or apparitions. When Jesus' name has been called upon, I have seen angels take that evil spirit and bind it with a chain. When I have seen that, I have thought, "God, how beautiful Your Word is to deliver these demon-possessed people from evil powers."

It is the Word of the Lord that works. It is Jesus Christ's Word. Only in His name—the name of Jesus Christ—will this work.

Call on the name of Jesus Christ. He will save you. You will be born again, set free from your sins, and have an eternal home in heaven.

THE POWER OF THE WORD

Once, I was in the country of Malaysia. The people were so hungry for the Lord, and I knew by the presence of God that there was going to be a mighty move of God. As the glory of God began to fall on us, it was like rain.

The Holy Spirit was moving in our midst and saving people. People were falling out of their seats to the ground as they accepted the Lord. Many souls were delivered as the Lord's power touched them. Oh, the joy and presence of

God that came down! The Word of God was being preached, and it was setting people free.

How the people hungered for God! They wanted to be born again and to ask Jesus Christ to come into their hearts. The power of the Word of God is incredible.

FOOD FOR THOUGHT

Here is another Scripture I would like you to think about:

> ¹⁹ *The Angel of God, who went before the camp of Israel, moved and went behind them; and the pillar of cloud went from before them and stood behind them.* ²⁰ *So it came between the camp of the Egyptians and the camp of Israel. Thus it was a cloud and darkness to the one, and it gave light by night to the other, so that the one did not come near the other all that night.*   (Exodus 14:19–20)

Children of God, don't you know that God wants to do miracles today just as He did yesterday? For some reason we have been eliminating the benefits God has provided for us. We have been neglecting all the beautiful things of God.

Psychics and all types of witchcraft and sorcery are in our land. They are speaking to the hunger in people's hearts. People are seeking advice and direction for their lives from all sources.

However, I am telling you that God is real and true. He does not want us to follow after psychics. He does not want to see the evils of witchcraft and the occult in the world.

God speaks against the occult and seeking after familiar spirits in His Word:

> [31] *Give no regard to mediums and familiar spirits; do not seek after them, to be defiled by them: I am the LORD your God.* (Leviticus 19:31)

It is very sinful and very wrong to go to mediums and psychics for help and guidance. Instead, God's angels are real and are sent to minister to us who are the heirs of salvation.

> [11] *For He shall give His angels charge over you, to keep you in all your ways.* (Psalm 91:11)

> [9] *In all their affliction He was afflicted, and the Angel of His Presence saved*

them; in His love and in His pity He re-deemed them; and He bore them and carried them all the days of old.

(Isaiah 63:9)

[28] *Nebuchadnezzar spoke, saying, "Blessed be the God of Shadrach, Me-shach, and Abed-Nego, who sent His Angel and delivered His servants who trusted in Him, and they have frus-trated the king's word, and yielded their bodies, that they should not serve nor worship any god except their own God!"*

(Daniel 3:28)

TROOPS OF ANGELS

When the Lord Jesus gave me a revelation of hell, I could see with my spiritual eyes that all around my home the Word of God was written in the sky.

Around and outside of my home was a great assemblage of angels. Some were sitting, talking among themselves. Another group had a very authoritative look and seemed to be watching. The angels in the third group around the house were standing wingtip to wingtip with their backs toward my home.

This last group was composed of the largest angels who all looked like warriors! Each had a large sword at his side. If even a dark shadow tried to creep toward my home, they would pull out their swords and defend my family.

Remember, *"the sword of the Spirit...is the word of God"* (Ephesians 6:17). The Word would come out blazing and go into the enemy. The enemy would be cremated and turned into ashes.

The Scripture came to me: *"The wicked... shall be ashes under the soles of your feet"* (Malachi 4:3). Seeing the Word of God in action continually amazed me.

When God sent His Word, the angels delivered Peter from prison:

> [7] *Now behold, an angel of the Lord stood by him, and a light shone in the prison; and he struck Peter on the side and raised him up, saying, "Arise quickly!" And his chains fell off his hands.*
> [8] *Then the angel said to him, "Gird yourself and tie on your sandals"; and so he did. And he said to him, "Put on your garment and follow me."*

⁹ *So he went out and followed him, and did not know that what was done by the angel was real, but thought he was seeing a vision.*

¹⁰ *When they were past the first and the second guard posts, they came to the iron gate that leads to the city, which opened to them of its own accord; and they went out and went down one street, and immediately the angel departed from him.*

¹¹ *And when Peter had come to himself, he said, "Now I know for certain that the Lord has sent His angel, and has delivered me from the hand of Herod and from all the expectation of the Jewish people."*   (Acts 12:7–11)

ANGELS AND THE WORD

We have many Scriptures where angels appeared to men. Some additional examples are:

²⁰ *But while he thought about these things, behold, an angel of the Lord appeared to him in a dream, saying, "Joseph, son of David, do not be afraid to take to you Mary your wife, for that which is conceived in her is of the Holy Spirit."*   (Matthew 1:20)

31 *Then the* LORD *opened Balaam's eyes, and he saw the angel of the* LORD *standing in the road with His sword drawn. So he bowed low and fell face down.*
(Numbers 22:31 NIV)

1 *So Jacob went on his way, and the angels of God met him.* (Genesis 32:1)

12 *And she saw two angels in white sitting, one at the head and the other at the feet, where the body of Jesus had lain.* (John 20:12)

26 *Now an angel of the Lord spoke to Philip, saying, "Arise and go toward the south along the road which goes down from Jerusalem to Gaza."*
(Acts 8:26)

23 *For there stood by me* [Paul] *this night an angel of the God to whom I belong and whom I serve.* (Acts 27:23)

As Christians we need to understand how much protection we have. We must understand that God has provided everything for us in His holy Word. When we need help, we can go to Him boldly in the time of need. At the throne of grace, in Jesus Christ's name, we ask Him for help.

When you and I ask for assistance, He always gives it. He loves to help us as we keep His commandments and serve Him.

Twelve

A New World Is Coming

For many days after my final sojourn in hell, I was desperately sick. I had to have the lights on when I slept. I needed the Bible with me at all times, and I read it constantly. My soul was in severe shock. I had experienced some of what the lost endure when they go to hell.

Jesus would say, *"Peace, be still!"* (Mark 4:39), and peace would flood my soul. Yet, within a few moments I would again be screaming, hysterical with fear.

During this time, I knew that I was never alone and that Jesus was always there. Nevertheless, even with that knowledge, I sometimes could not feel His presence. Sometimes I was so afraid of having to go back to hell that I was fearful to even have Jesus near me.

When I tried to tell others about my experiences in hell, they would not listen to me. I begged them, "Please, repent of your sins before it's too late." It was difficult for anyone to believe what I told them about the torment that I had endured, as well as what Jesus had told me to write about hell.

The Lord reassured me that He was the Lord who heals. Even though I was not convinced I would ever fully recover, complete healing did come, slowly but surely.

PARADISE OF PEACE

And then it happened again. Again I was with the Lord Jesus, and we were soaring high up in the sky.

Jesus said, "I want to show you the love and goodness of God and parts of heaven. I want you to see the wondrous works of the Lord, which are so beautiful to behold."

An angel met us and said to me, "See the goodness and kindness of the Lord your God. His mercy endures forever."

There was such a sense of love and tenderness about the angel that I was about to weep when he spoke again, "Behold the power and might and majesty of God. Let me show you the place He has created for the children."

Suddenly, there was a large planet looming before us, a planet that appeared to be as large as the earth.

> [1] *Now I saw a new heaven and a new earth, for the first heaven and the first earth had passed away. Also there was no more sea.*
> [2] *Then I, John, saw the holy city, New Jerusalem, coming down out of heaven from God, prepared as a bride adorned for her husband.* (Revelation 21:1-2)

The next thing I heard was the voice of the Father saying,

The Father, the Son, and the Holy Spirit are all one. The Father and the Son are one, and the Father and the Holy Spirit are one. I sent My Son to die on a cross so that no one needs to be lost.

I am about to show you the place I made for My children. I care greatly about all children. I care when a mother loses a child, even as the fruit of your womb was cast before its time. You see, I know all things, and I care.

From the time there is life in the womb, I know. I know about the babies that are murdered while they are still in their mother's bodies—the aborted lives that are cut off and unwanted. I know about the stillborn and those children who are born with crippling defects. From the time of conception, each is a soul.

My angels go down and bring the children to Me when they die. In heaven they are loved, and they become perfect beings. I give them whole bodies and restore whatever parts are missing. I give them perfected bodies.

All over the planet there was a feeling of being loved, a sense of perfect well-being. Everything was perfect. Here and there amid the lush green grass and pools of crystal clear water were marble seats and highly polished wooden benches to sit on.

Everywhere I looked, there were children engaged in all kinds of activities. Each child wore a spotless white robe and sandals. The white robes were so bright that they glistened in the magnificent light on the planet. A profusion of color everywhere accented the whiteness of the children's robes. Angels were the keepers of the entrance, and the children's names were all written in a book.

I saw children learning the Word of God and being taught music from a golden book. I was surprised to see animals of all sorts coming up to the children or sitting beside them while they were in this angelic school.

There were no tears and no sorrow. Everything was supremely beautiful. Joy and happiness were everywhere.

Then the angel showed me another planet that glowed like a great light before me. The light shone with the radiance of a million stars, and everything on the planet was beautiful and alive. In the distance I saw two mountains made of pure gold, while closer to me were two golden gates, in which diamonds and other precious stones were embedded.

I knew in my heart that this was the new earth and that the city lying in splendor before me was the New Jerusalem—the city of God as it will come down to earth.

EARTH AGAIN

Quickly, I was back viewing the old earth, but the earth as it will be after the Great Tribulation but before the final fires of Armageddon will ultimately purge it. In this scene, too, I saw Jerusalem, the capital city of the millennium.

In my vision, I saw people coming from far and near, making their way toward this city. Here Jesus was King, and all the nations of the earth brought Him gifts and paid Him homage. Not only was He King in fact, He was also recognized as King of Kings!

Jesus gave me the interpretation of my vision and gave me greater clarity about what will happen then:

Soon I will return and take back with Me to heaven the righteous dead first. Then after them, those who are alive and remain will be caught up to be with Me in the air.

Following that, the Antichrist will reign upon the earth for an appointed time, and there will be tribulations such as have never been before, nor will ever be again.

And then I will return with My saints, and Satan will be cast into the bottomless pit, where he will remain for a thousand years. During that thousand years, I will reign over the earth from Jerusalem.

When the Millennium is past, Satan will be released for a season, and I will defeat him by the brightness of My coming. The old earth will pass away.

Behold, there shall be a new earth and a New Jerusalem coming down upon it, and I will reign forever and ever.

Thirteen

The Return of Christ

In another vision, I saw the coming of the Lord! I heard His call like the sound of a trumpet and the voice of an archangel (1 Thessalonians 4:16). The whole earth shook, and out of the graves came the righteous dead to meet their Lord in the air.

For what seemed like hours, I heard the trumpets blaring. The earth and the sea gave up their dead (Revelation 20:13). The Lord Jesus

Christ stood atop the clouds in vestments of fire and beheld the glorious scene.

I heard the sound of trumpets again. As I watched, those who were alive and remained on the earth ascended to meet them:

> 14 *If we believe that Jesus died and rose again, even so God will bring with Him those who sleep in Jesus.*
> 15 *For this we say to you by the word of the Lord, that we who are alive and remain until the coming of the Lord will by no means precede those who are asleep.*
> 16 *For the Lord Himself will descend from heaven with a shout, with the voice of an archangel, and with the trumpet of God. And the dead in Christ will rise first.*
> 17 *Then we who are alive and remain shall be caught up together with them in the clouds to meet the Lord in the air. And thus we shall always be with the Lord.* (1 Thessalonians 4:14–17)

I saw the redeemed, as millions of points of light, converging on a gathering place in the sky. There the angels gave them robes of purest white. There was great rejoicing.

It was the angels' responsibility to serve, and they were everywhere, giving special attention to the risen ones. New glorified bodies were given to the redeemed, and they were transformed as they passed through the air.

Great joy and happiness filled the heavens, and the angels sang, "Glory to the King of Kings!"

THE BODY OF CHRIST

In this vision, I beheld a large spiritual body high in the heavens. It was the body of Christ, which was lying on its back while blood dripped to the earth. I knew this represented our Lord's slain body. The body grew larger and larger until it encompassed the heavens. Going into it were millions of redeemed saints.

I watched in astonishment as millions climbed up a staircase to the body and filled it, beginning with the feet and continuing through the legs, the arms, the stomach, the heart, and the head.

When it was full, I saw that it was filled with people from all corners of the earth. With a mighty voice they praised the Lord:

> 9 *And they sang a new song, saying:*
> *"You are worthy to take the scroll, and*
> *to open its seals; for You were slain, and*
> *have redeemed us to God by Your blood*
> *out of every tribe and tongue and people*
> *and nation,*
> 10 *"and have made us kings and priests*
> *to our God; and we shall reign on the*
> *earth."*   (Revelation 5:9–10)

Millions were gathered before the throne, and I saw angels as they brought the books from which judgment was read. There was the mercy seat, and rewards were given to many.

Then, as I watched in astonishment, darkness covered the face of the earth, and demon forces went everywhere. Countless evil spirits had been loosed from their prison and spilled forth onto the earth. I heard another loud voice saying,

> 12 *Woe to the inhabitants of the earth*
> *and the sea! For the devil has come*
> *down to you, having great wrath, be-*
> *cause he knows that he has a short time.*
>   (Revelation 12:12)

THE WRATH OF GOD

I saw an angry beast, and he poured out his venom upon all the earth. Hell shook in his fury, and from a bottomless pit came swarming hordes of evil creatures to blacken the earth with their vast numbers.

Men and women ran crying into the hills, the caves, and the mountains. And there were wars upon the earth, and famine and death.

At last I saw horses and chariots of fire in the heavens. The earth trembled, while *"the sun became black as sackcloth of hair, and the moon became like blood"* (Revelation 6:12).

An angel announced, "Hear, O earth, the King is coming!"

Then the King of Kings and the Lord of Lords appeared in the sky. With Him in glorious splendor were the saints of all ages, clad in purest white. I remembered that *"every eye will see Him"* (Revelation 1:7) and that *"every knee shall bow...and every tongue shall confess"* (Romans 14:11) that He is Lord.

Then the angels put in their sickles and harvested the ripened grain (see Revelation

14:14–19), which is the end of the world.

I thought, "We must love one another. We must be firm in the truth and correct our children in the light of the soon coming of Christ. For surely, the King is coming!"

Fourteen

The Lord's Final Plea: Be Ready

Jesus said to me, "Repent and be saved, for the kingdom of God is at hand. My will and My Word will be performed. Prepare the way of the Lord." Then He declared:

> *"Command those who are rich in this present age not to be haughty, nor to trust in uncertain riches but in the living God, who gives us richly all things to enjoy"* (1 Timothy 6:17).

195

Tell them to walk in the Spirit, and they will not fulfill the lust of the flesh (Galatians 5:16). *"Do not be deceived, God is not mocked; for whatever a man sows, that he will also reap. For he who sows to his flesh will of the flesh reap corruption, but he who sows to the Spirit will of the Spirit reap everlasting life"* (Galatians 6:7–8).

"Now the works of the flesh are evident, which are: adultery, fornication, uncleanness, lewdness, idolatry, sorcery, hatred, contentions, jealousies, outbursts of wrath, selfish ambitions, dissensions, heresies, envy, murders, drunkenness, revelries, and the like; of which I tell you beforehand, just as I also told you in time past, that those who practice such things will not inherit the kingdom of God. But the fruit of the Spirit is love, joy, peace, longsuffering, kindness, goodness, faithfulness, gentleness, self-control. Against such there is no law. And those who are [Mine] *have crucified the flesh with its passions and desires"* (Galatians 5:19–24).

Jesus continued:

When the Word of God is fulfilled, then the end will come. No man knows the day or the hour when the Son of God will return to the earth. Not even the Son knows, for that is known only by the Father.

The Word is quickly being fulfilled. Come as a little child, and let Me cleanse you from the works of the flesh.

Say to Me, "Lord Jesus, come into my heart and forgive me of my sins. I know that I am a sinner, and I repent of my sins. Wash me in Your blood, and make me clean. I have sinned against heaven and before You and am not worthy to be called a son. I receive You by faith as my Savior."

I will give you pastors after My own heart, and I will be your Shepherd. You will be My people, and I will be your God. Read the Word, and do not forsake the assembling of yourselves together. Give your whole life to Me, and I will keep you. I will never leave or forsake you.

BE READY TO MEET GOD

Dear ones, from the depths of my heart, I have shared with you many of the visions and revelations of heaven that were given to me by the power of God Almighty. I want to sum up my thoughts by expressing how much God loves us. He has shown His care and great love by sending forth His mighty Word to us and granting us revelations in these last days.

Dear children, we must be ready to meet the Lord. We must at all times be looking for His coming. You and I know the troubles, the times, and the season we are in. There has never been an era like this.

With all my heart I urge you to be ready, *"for you know neither the day nor the hour in which the Son of Man is coming"* (Matthew 25:13). Jesus Christ is coming back!

Do you remember how I talked about the saints who are now in heaven? The angel of God told me that if we live righteously in Christ Jesus, we will meet our loved ones at the gates of glory as we go in.

Are you receiving this beautiful message in your heart?

I talked about the books and records that the angels keep. Everything we do for Jesus' sake is recorded, and our rewards are going to be much greater in heaven than they are on the earth. Angels write down our deeds.

Many times evangelists, preachers, teachers, and other leaders have to temporarily leave homes, children, and spouses to carry the cross for Jesus Christ. The Lord sees this, and He knows all about it.

He also knows about the many times we go somewhere and are not treated like children of the Lord. Sometimes we are mistreated, but we are still the King's kids.

Still, God wants us to be servants to servants. He wants us to serve one another as He served us.

Saints, God didn't promise us a rose garden. Although He didn't promise us splendor down here, we can have blessings, riches, honor, and material things as God permits. However, we can have them as we take up our crosses and follow Christ.

I want you to be ready. If you have never received Jesus Christ as your Lord and Savior, you can be saved, according to the Holy Scriptures:

16 For God so loved the world that He gave His only begotten Son, that whoever believes in Him should not perish but have everlasting life. (John 3:16)

9 If you confess with your mouth the Lord Jesus and believe in your heart that God has raised Him from the dead, you will be saved.
10 For with the heart one believes unto righteousness, and with the mouth confession is made unto salvation.
13 Whoever calls on the name of the LORD shall be saved.

(Romans 10:9–10, 13)

Please pray this prayer right now:

Father, in the name of Jesus Christ, I come unto You, just as I am. I am a sinner, Lord. I have sinned against You and against heaven. I ask You, Lord Jesus, to forgive me and to come into my heart and save my soul. Let me be born again by the Spirit of the Living God.

I give my life to You, Lord Jesus. I do believe that You are the Son of God. I believe You are Jesus Christ who was sent to save my soul from hell. I give You thanks and praise and honor for redeeming me by Your precious blood.

If you have prayed this prayer with me and really believed what you prayed, you are now saved. You have asked Jesus Christ into your heart. Begin to confess Him with your lips and praise Him.

To God be all praise and honor!

About the Author

Mary Kathryn Baxter was born in Chatta-nooga, Tennessee. She was brought up in the house of God. While she was still young, her mother taught her about Jesus Christ and His salvation.

Kathryn was born again at the age of nineteen. After serving the Lord for several years, she backslid for a season. The Spirit of the Lord would not release her, and she came back and gave her life anew to Christ. She still serves Him faithfully.

In the mid-1960s Kathryn moved with her family to Detroit, Michigan, where she lived for a time. She later moved to Belleville, Michigan, where she began to have visions from God.

Ministers, leaders, and saints of the Lord speak very highly of her and her ministry. The movement of the Holy Spirit is emphasized in all her services, and many miracles have occurred in them. The gifts of the Holy Spirit with demonstrations of power are manifested in her meetings as she is led by the Spirit of God. She loves the Lord with all her heart, mind, soul, and strength and desires above all else to be a soulwinner for Jesus Christ.

Kathryn has been married for more than twenty-eight years to Bill Baxter. They have four children and six grandchildren, who support her in the ministry.

She is truly a dedicated handmaiden of the Lord. Her calling is specifically in the area of dreams, visions, and revelations. She was ordained as a minister in 1983 at the Full Gospel Church of God in Taylor, Michigan. She now ministers with the National Church of God in Washington, D.C.

In 1976, while she was living in Belleville, Jesus appeared to her in human form, in dreams, in visions, and in revelations. Since that time she has received many visitations from the Lord. During those visits He has shown her the depths, degrees, levels, and torments of lost souls in hell. She has also received many visions of heaven, the Great Tribulation, and the end of time.

During one period of her life, Jesus appeared to her each night for forty nights. He revealed to her the horrors of hell and the glories of heaven. He told her that this message is for the whole world.

ORDER FORM
Mary K. Baxter

A Divine Revelation of Hell

Item	Quantity	Price Per Item	TOTAL
Book- English		$10.99	$
Book - Spanish		$ 9.99	$
1 Single Tape (English or Spanish)		$10.99	$
2 Tape Album (English)		$15.99	$
2 Tape Album (Spanish)		$15.99	$
Newest Release: A Divine Revelation of Heaven			
Book- English		$10.99	$
For each item, please add $2.00 for shipping and handling		$ 2.00	$
TOTAL AMOUNT ENCLOSED			$

____Cash   ____Check   ____Money Order

____VISA   ____MasterCard

Signature_____

Card # _____ Expiration Date _____

Mail to: National Christian Booksellers
6700 Bock Road, Ft. Washington, Md., 20744
(301) 567-9500

--ORDER FORM--
Dr. T.L. Lowery
Books - Audio Tapes - Video Tapes

	Quantity	TOTAL
AUDIO TAPES		
Two-Tape Series .... **$10.00 Each**		
Eagle Saints/ Possessing Your Possessions	_____	_____
Fruit of the Spirit.................	_____	_____
Lame Man That Leaped, The/ Look and Live...................................	_____	_____
Our Royal Heritage/ Preach Jesus.................	_____	_____
Qualifications for the Rapture/ God Has An Appointment With You.........	_____	_____
Seven Names of God/ Seven Blessings of Being in Christ....................	_____	_____
Things Unshakable/ Steadfast Faith.................	_____	_____
Things We Must Not Lose/ Lest I Become a Castaway......................	_____	_____
When The Russian Bear Meets The Lion of the Tribe of Judah/		
After Armageddon What then?........................	_____	_____
Four-Tape Series...........................**$20.00 Each**		
Iraq in Bible Prophesy.................	_____	_____
Principles of Total Christian Stewardship, The................................	_____	_____
Spiritual Gifts.................	_____	_____
Financial Freedom.................	_____	_____
VIDEO TAPES...............................**$20.00 Each**		
Dynamic Christian Leadership................................	_____	_____
God's Royal Heritage.................	_____	_____
Prayers of Paul, The.................	_____	_____
BOOKS ....**$6.95 Each**		
The Baptism of the Holy Ghost.................	_____	_____
Come Quickly Lord Jesus.................	_____	_____
Holy Spirit at Work, The.................	_____	_____
Next World Dictator, The.................	_____	_____
Power Plus.................	_____	_____
BOOKS ....**$8.95 Each**		
Prayers that Prevail.................	_____	_____
The Hem of His Garment.................	_____	_____

Newest Book Release
Gifted to Serve.................................$10.99 Each _____

Total Amount $_____

*Please add $2.00 per item for shipping ($2.00) $_____

TOTAL AMOUNT ENCLOSED $_____

__Cash   __Check   __Money Order   __VISA   __MasterCard

Signature_____

Card#_____Expiration Date_____

Mail to: National Christian Booksellers
6700 Bock Rd., Ft. Washington, Md. 20744 --(301) 567-9500